TAUGHT HOW TO LOVE BY WOLVES

Healing from improper relationships and regaining your identity

Edition One

Crystal Jackson

Books may be purchased in quantity and/or special sales
by contacting the publisher, Crystal Jackson, at
P.O. Box 684 Eustis, FL 32727; or by visiting website
http://www.anointingonfire.org/books-and-skits.html

Taught How to Love by Wolves: Healing from
improper relationships and regaining your identity
ISBN-13: 978-1537639956
ISBN-10: 1537639951

DEDICATION

I dedicate this book to the Heavenly Father, the Son and the Holy Spirit.

My inspiration to write this book came from them. They have enabled, empowered and comforted me during many tears while writing this book. They are the reason I've endured the wolves encountered throughout my journey and the reason I am alive to say, "I am a wolf overcomer." Many of you will be wolf overcomers because of them also.

I also dedicate the book to the freedom of those who are or once were amongst wolves. Thank God for your freedom. The very thought of your freedom has empowered me to write nonstop many days. You're so special to me. Breathtaking.

I love you dearly.

CONTENTS

FOREWORD

In Taught How to Love by Wolves, readers will receive a source of wisdom, hope, spiritual enlightenment, encouragement & spiritual stamina. This is a book that holds many keys to spiritual deliverance and divine healing. This book was birthed from many years of heart ache and pain, but through it all Crystal Jackson was able to overcome the wolves. In her times of weakness, God's strength was made perfect in her. Please allow this book to impart total deliverance and healing in every area of your life.
--Apostle Bettye Lovett
Pastor & Overseer
Faith Healing & Anointing Temple
Tallahassee, FL

PREFACE

I was brought from my mom's womb into wolf environment and territory. My dad was taught how to love by wolves and never healed, so he didn't love my mom or the mother of my sisters and brothers properly. When you're not healed yourself from improper relationships, you cannot love others properly. Bringing children into the world on a foundation of adultery and sexual sins gives an open door to the spirit of segregation.

I can imagine the struggle my ancestors and grandparents endured at a time when segregation was much worse than now. Back then this spirit of segregation (and still today) used a color to operate and express hatred, causing segregation in the lives of many. This spirit is so crafty; it operates in many ways.

Because my childhood environment was the territory of wolves, my half-brothers and half-sisters that I grew up and at times lived in the same home with did not have a proper loving relationship with my full sibling and me. Our environment and territory growing up was so dysfunctional and unstable. Deep down we love each other, but being amongst wolves automatically teaches you a different way to love and think.

13

The wolf environment and territory was so severe, directly in result of the spirit of segregation at operation through my generational line. This spirit has not been faced as it should be, nor with the urgency that it needs. It causes separation, grief and dysfunctional homes or family life. It squeezes happiness out from the very ones that you love.

This spirit can hide and cause you to look at each other as the problem while it causes confusion and hatred. It's so desperate it loves even to operate within marriages. It brings separation in marriages and causes spouses, although together, to live apart. It causes mates not to be able to choose one mate, keeps dishonesty and loves to keep one from living as they desire, always going the opposite way they intended. This spirit is an enemy to my family that will be taken down. Enough is enough.

There will be a man that rises on fire for God, sold out to God's agenda. He will be totally sold out to the desire of his flesh and love his wife as Christ loves the Church. There will be no distrust or misuse in their marriage and he will not stray from faithfulness, keeping his marriage bed pure. He will be a man that discovers his wife when she has discovered her identity in Christ Jesus, one which disallows the spirit of segregation to operate.

There will be a woman who raises her sons and daughters in the will of God, one that breaks down the wall that has been formed by the enemy. This wall was formed using the spirit of segregation but will be brought down to the ground so that the foundation is destroyed. It shall fall and be consumed, and all those of my generation current and who are to come will know that the Heavenly Father is Lord.

Due to the overbearing weight of the dysfunction in my home I left at the age of 15 and got married. The desire for normalness and to please others drew me into the arms of a family of wolves. I was hurting from seeing hatefulness a child should never see. I had seen much abuse done to my mother, to the point of being dedicated to revenge for the wrong done to her. Secretly, the enemy was using this wrong dedication to cause me to come into marriage with those God never intended for me. I could no longer stand to see the mistreatment; I had to get away.

It is my belief that many others now or at some point attempted to obtain revenge, knowingly or unknowingly, for the mistreatment of their mother or a loved one. I have learned we are not to make right the wrong done to our loved ones. Only God can correct this and reveal what we do not know. The environment and territory of wolves caused me to marry young and run straight into a family of wolves, but I couldn't go home for help because it too was a territory of wolves. I did try but was reminded of why I left home in the first place.

I had to live amongst the wolves to gain my freedom. In this process, I was running from one wolf into the arms of another much cleverer and better-dressed wolf. It hurts because I could not rely upon any of my family- all of whom, in my opinion, had been taught how to love by wolves or from the environment or territory of the wolves.

I have endured to tell my story of the wisdom gained in result of the many improper relationships- coworkers, professional, romantic, sibling, friendships and the list goes on. Some relationships were entered voluntarily, many involuntarily. So I wrote this book so you may avoid wolves, or endure and outlast the manners learned automatically amongst wolves to tell your story.

To those that are amongst wolves, voluntarily or involuntarily, I wrote this book so that family members will understand you. And just in case you don't have a family or anyone to help you come from amongst the wolves, I am writing the second edition for you. I had to obtain my freedom from the wolves without family or friends.

I have written this book to release insight, knowledge, understanding and encouragement on how to deal with those that have been taught how to love by wolves.

It is for you who does not understand a loved one or child who is in a bad relationship or situation and, although you can see the way they can escape, your loved one does not seem to see it or understand how important it is to leave with urgency. Learn to understand them and get answers to the *why* questions. Recognize how to help them, what to do and what NOT to do.

To the friends of a loved one who don't understand why they just won't leave a relationship that clearly isn't good, I write and dedicate to you. S/he does want to get out and s/he is listening each time you talk, but it's hard to leave from amongst the wolves, especially when you've been there so long. You can't just get up and go, even when the coast looks clear.

For those whose loved ones are in a gang or hanging with the wrong crowd, yes, they do want out; they think about it, fantasize how it would be if they had never been a part of the gang or the wrong crowd or if they were free; it's hard to leave from amongst the wolves.

To those suffering spousal abuse, I dedicate this book also to you. Yes, you keep going back, and no, you don't like being mistreated or beaten. I write to tell your loved one that yes, you do want help to get out but don't know how. The situation isn't normal. You feel you should be able to just get up and go, but it doesn't always work like that and you live to tell the story when you are amongst the wolves. You're in danger anytime you think of freedom and the wolves find out, so while you think of freedom you act as if you don't want freedom to survive and to stay alive.

For that person who is struggling in an improper loving relationship, I know you dream of your freedom. I know what it feels like to get the courage to go, then face the circumstances and become discouraged again- the consistent replay and thoughts of those who love to say, "I told you so." I know what it feels like to just stay rather than deal with the unpleasant "welcome home." You've got it in you to win and you will claim your freedom, but I also understand that it's hard to escape amongst the wolves.

This book will equip Pastors with how to reach those that are not so easily understood, those seemingly withdrawn, seemingly asking for help and not asking at the same time.

For the spouse who doesn't understand how their mate can be so loving at times and so dogmatic at other times or so insecure, this book will help you understand the battle your mate may have endured and the healing process they are undergoing or still must navigate. Learn to understand their process to freedom and get the freedom that is very necessary for you. See how you must be strong and endure as a good soldier.

This book is also for you whose marriage has endured hard times (such as infidelity) and who needs healing. You need healing after such an occurrence; you must learn to love correctly, whether you stayed or left or will stay or leave. You must overcome what is necessary so that your life does not get stuck where you are. You must overcome fears or insecurity and heal to love correctly.

This book is for those that have been amongst the wolves for so long that it has taught you to love so cautiously that you've nearly lost your true identity. It is for those who are amongst the wolves right now, trapped, wanting to run but can't, wanting to ask for help, needing help, wanting help but unable to ask.

This book brings awareness to those that have been taught how to love by wolves and equips them to deal with their current situations. It acknowledges the process and brings greater understanding of those in or who were once in unfulfilling and unhealthy relationships, situations or environments.

It is for those who do not know where to begin telling their story and who don't know how to ask for help without telling too much. Indeed, you don't like telling so much once you've lived amongst wolves; you learn that wolves use what you say to hurt you deeper. To avoid this, you seem to automatically pick up the manner of withholding expression of self to avoid being hurt further, but in normal healthy environments and relationships, you are appreciated and affirmed for expressing yourself.

I encourage you: don't be afraid to ask for the help you need. Opening your mouth at the right time and with the right people releases empowerment that leads to freedom. Let's take the journey to being in that place of true expression. Truth promotes healing and leads to more truth, and while you come into embracing truth, freedom comes. I welcome you to the freedom you deserved so long ago.

ACKNOWLEDGMENTS

Special thank you to my daughter's A'Lena and Ja'Leah Koonce. May this book bless you. You've allowed me to fully perceive the significance of loving one as if they have already arrived having no stains, blemishes or wrinkles. You both empower me to reach, release and grab what I must. Love you dearly.

Grateful thank you to my sons Jaheim and Drease Wiley, who fuel me with consistent inspiration and prayers not just in writing this book. Thank you and love you dearly.

Thank you to Patricia Stoddard, who gives the invitation for realness, honesty and truthfulness. This attitude helps me to discover more of my identity and continue to be a strong warrior when times are tough. Thank you for not only being a sister but friend and counselor.

Thank you to Chantelle Smith for proofreading with such quickness.

Gracious thank you to Apostle Betty Lovett and my church family at Faith Healing and Anointing Temple in Tallahassee, FL, who accepted me and my family with open arms and many prayers. Love you all dearly.

Special thank you to the editor for her patience and persistence to cause this book to become no longer a dream but reality.

PART 1: WHAT IT MEANS TO BE TAUGHT TO LOVE BY WOLVES

WHO THE WOLVES ARE

As I struggled with the conviction that I must write this book, I questioned God: *were the readers of this book going to understand the title?* God's reply to me was that throughout the bible, characteristics of animals were used to gain understanding or to grasp fully the meaning of the parables shared.

After God had spoken this I looked up some of the bible verses (King James Version - KJV). I would like to share them with you as we prepare for this journey of discovering truth and awareness of where you are right now. I hope you can use the verses to obtain the help you need to move to a healthier state (or to assist a loved one in doing so).

> **Psalm 22:13** *They gaped upon me with their mouths, as a ravening and a roaring lion.*
> Here David compares his adversaries to a roaring lion that rips its prey.
>
> **Psalm 22:21** *Save me from the lion's mouth: for thou hast heard me from the horns of the unicorns.*

Genesis 49:27 *Benjamin shall ravin* as *a wolf: in the morning he shall devour the prey, and at night he shall divide the spoil.*

Isaiah 11:6 *The wolf also shall dwell with the lamb, and the leopard shall lie down with the kid; and the calf and the young lion and the fatling together; and a little child shall lead them.*

Isaiah 65:25 *The wolf and the lamb shall feed together, and the lion shall eat straw like the bullock; and dust* shall be *the serpent's meat. They shall not hurt nor destroy in all my holy mountain, saith the LORD.*

Jeremiah 5:6 *Wherefore a lion out of the forest shall slay them,* and *a wolf of the evenings shall spoil them, a leopard shall watch over their cities: every one that goeth out thence shall be torn in pieces: because their transgressions are many,* and *their backslidings are increased.*

Matthew 7:15 *Beware of false prophets, which come to you in sheep's clothing, but inwardly they are ravening wolves.*

In this book, "the wolves" is a reference to the ways of the wolves, the manner that they seek out their prey and how they wait for the right time to expose their real intent and true desire. Wolves are sly and very intelligent in gaining what they want; they study their prey and use strategy to bring that prey into subjection. Discussion of "the wolves" includes any situation that is presented at first as great and then later involves the true motivation surfacing. You realize the person, situation, circumstances, deal or the environment was not great at all.

I remember encountering the first wolf; I met him during my teenage years. Regaining freedom would be tough. I remember the wolf's presentation was great. (Wolves are great at creating picture shows and acting them out. Picture shows are false images that they want to plant in your thinking as part of the plot to bring you to subjection, to get what they want. Wolves come with motives from the very beginning but are good at hiding them.)

This wolf presented himself as a shining light: wanted to help me, ready to be there, understanding, ready to go all the way, a ride or die partner, vowed for better or worse. But (there is always a but when dealing with wolves), once he believed I was far enough away from those that loved me or those that supported me and had influence in my life, the wolf began to show that he was a wolf.

The entire time, he had been mapping out the stage and preparing the kill, planning to steal the very life out of me. This was not just a baby wolf; this wolf's strategy had come from much experience. I was so hurt. This was not a friend; this was a well-dressed wolf in sheep's clothing.

The truth is that many of us have been, will be one day, are right now, or have a loved one who has been or is amongst the wolves. This is why it is important that you are able to identify those that have been amongst the wolves or who are now; the manner in which you respond matters greatly. Your response to those amongst or recently amongst wolves has to be different than someone that isn't amongst the wolves or has never been.

Many parents are losing children to suicide and freak accidents; circumstances haven't been addressed according to the child's state. The children do not know they are amongst the wolves (most adults do not, until they are already in deeply); if you as parents are not able to identify when your child is amongst wolves, it can cost you greatly. You must know which stage amongst the wolves they are in, to know how to communicate with the loved one.

Many pastors become tired or give up and label a struggling individual as someone who doesn't want to be free or as someone rejecting what

Jesus has for them; this is often the result of failure to identify them as someone that came from amongst wolves. They are not crazy; they have to be healed because they still function as if they are amongst the wolves.

It is important that we teach our loved ones what a wolf looks like, smells like and portrays itself to be. This reminds me of the childhood story, *Little Red Riding Hood*. The wolf knew that Little Red Riding Hood had goods and wanted them. The wolf mapped out a way to get her goods, watching and planning without her realizing; he was clever and very sly. He came up with a plan to disguise himself to look as Little Red Riding Hood's grandmother, who was sick. The wolf spotted her while on the journey to take her grandmother some treats and preyed upon her. You have to read the rest of this story, *The Little Red Riding Hood,* for yourself. This is exactly what the wolves do; they blend in to camouflage and sneak in unnoticed. I like to say they like to creep, and say "Peek-a- boo, I got you."

You must notice what wolves say out of their mouths; these are the biggest clues. Evaluate what a person says; hold it captive to what the Father in Heaven knows, because no one knows you or your purpose like He does. Do whatever the Father says no matter what you think you know. This is how we get amongst the wolves anyways- thinking we got it, not holding all concerns big and small captive to what He knows already.

Paying close attention to what amuses a person helps you identify wolves. Watch very closely what entertains a person. If you are dating, and a person loves to watch a show about cheaters, and it thrills them how someone gets away with cheating, be warned. This couldn't hold their interest in this way unless something on the inside had a pull toward this. What's inside sooner or later comes out; it cannot hide forever.

The experience of dealing with wolves helps you become very great at discerning them. Just a couple of words and a little time spent and it's like your inner being just has a knowing. I like to say that you can smell them from afar. Keep reading; if you can't already you will be able to smell them from afar as well. That is one of the goals of writing this book to you.

HOW WE ARE TAUGHT TO LOVE
BY WOLVES

Taught how to love by wolves definitely doesn't mean that a person is heartless. It just refers to a person's situation, circumstance or environment; it refers to what they have accepted as love, entertained to be love or associated with love, be it a bad relationship, a drug addiction, unethical job or deal, or association with people who don't love you in return. Taught how to love by wolves simply means to be in an environment amongst people who do not properly love you, people who were dressed as sheep to hide wolfish characteristics.

The adjustment of being around wolves, the consistent disappointment and having to think in survival mode begin to teach you a different way to love. You become very cautious with giving of yourself and loving freely. Once you're in deep enough the wolves expose who they truly are, then it's not so easy to leave. You have a fight. This fight most often makes no sense to others, and you may be referred to as stupid and crazy by those who do not understand what it is like being amongst wolves. Being in such unhealthy environments, you automatically learn different manners to survive to make it through the day. When you finally come into a place of being healed, you have to be renewed

33

in your thinking because you've learned in most cases to love improperly and developed wrong thinking, especially of self.

One of the things that you learn automatically when amongst wolves is to hide how you really feel. When you have blended with the wolves for long periods, you have to learn who you are for yourself. Amongst wolves, you can lose yourself trying to blend or having no choice but to blend in order to survive from the wolves attempting to kill you (there are even some amongst the wolves who desire to kill themselves).

Some who are amongst the wolves become afraid to give without hiding that they are giving. To give freely is a great desire when you are amongst wolves, but giving is credited as nothing; it's not appreciated even when you've given your last. Giving all your heart gets you the return of nothing at all. Your natural development kicks in; you can't stop giving when that's just who you are, but automatically you begin giving in a way that does not place much attention on what you've given, as if it is nothing.

Amongst wolves one is taught unhealthy ways of thinking and a skewed view point of what true love is. This must change. It is challenging to live amongst wolves; it's not easy coming from wrong thinking. You must understand that you are valuable and that your time is precious. Those of you taught how to love by wolves must learn to add up your true worth and understand that your presence alone makes a difference in the lives of those that deserve your time. You must learn that you can give with purity and without fear to those you love. Some will have to stop seeking affirmations before stepping out into new things. The bible tells us about perfect love.

> *1 John 4:18 (KJV)*
> *There is no fear in love; but perfect love casteth out fear: because fear hath torment. He that feareth is not made perfect in love.*

Those taught how to love by wolves love with fear of being hurt and lack of expression; great things are not expressed because one amongst wolves knows happiness is short lived. Each person is different, so you must map out all the things that changed since their free expression of pure love. Those taught how to love by wolves automatically build walls, which I call rebellion to God. These walls must come down.

Once you build walls you have said, *I am going to fix it myself*; *No one will ever hurt me or do this to me every again*. You have taken it upon yourself to fix the problem. The bible says that apart from the Father we can do nothing. God is trying to get us to a point where we will rely on him, not ourselves. I am not saying you should not believe in yourself. What I am saying is that we must lean not unto our own understanding of things. God can heal us; we are to go about things His way, leaning on God's understanding.

When we do lean on Him, He shows us things we haven't seen although they were directly in front of us the entire time. He tells and shows us things that we never knew about ourselves. He begins to heal and restore us, and the best thing is that He keeps us from falling into the enemy's traps again by doing things His way. He sees all and knows all; we don't see all nor do we know all. So trust God for healing your pain and to not get back in to the same things we desire not to.

Some of the walls we build even keep us from loving ourselves and/ or forgiving ourselves. These walls keep bitterness and anger pent up inside and hidden. God never wanted the walls. Some cannot love their children properly because they are afraid of being hurt; they are afraid of the pain they may experience by letting people in and loving freely without the feeling that they will be hurt in return for the love they give.

THE DANGER IN LOVING
AS IF STILL AMONGST WOLVES

Those that truly love you will love you
unconditionally. It's sad when we still love them
with our guards up as if we are still amongst the
wolves. The danger in this is that you are
hurting yourself and hurting them; you push
them away at a time you need them the most.
This is tiresome, draining, and unhealthy for a
person that loves you; they may feel like they've
done something wrong consistently. Those who
are (or recently were) amongst wolves love
very cautiously, not giving freely what is
required in the relationship. Some never open
up to what now is true love; the danger is that
they may push this true love away. It's like
tearing your own home down after you've
worked so hard to build it up.

Loving as if you are still amongst wolves steals
potential greatness and causes the lack of joy
and happiness that you and those amongst you
truly deserve. This is like locking them up in a
prison to suffer as if it's a secret. You hold love
back from someone that truly deserves your
love. Your way of thinking needs healing; you
give love to those who do not love you in return
without question, but now someone loves you
in return and you hold back, questioning
everything. You miss out on things God really all

along intended for you and you take from the joy with your stinky thinking; this is why it is dangerous. Trying to love them as if you are still amongst the wolves suffocates life out of the goodness you have. You must step outside of the hurt; forget those who hurt you, so that the hurt can stop you from taking it everywhere you go. If you can remember like yesterday what someone has done to you in the past, that's the sign you need to heal.

When you fail to properly love those that truly love you, you love and then pull back, which is not good. It's like teasing a baby with a piece of candy and then yanking it back. You know the baby wants the candy, but once the baby reaches out for the candy you yank it back. This is hurtful to those that truly love you; they do not want to hurt you but love you.

If your loved one was indeed taught to love amongst wolves, I pray for you to stand strong with them because most of the time they do not know of their stinky thinking. They think they are protecting themselves and that their way of thinking is protection from hurt; their way of thinking has to be renewed.

ENDURING AS A GOOD SOLDIER

Why it's important to endure as a good soldier for those once or presently amongst the wolves.

It will not be a piece of cake dealing with someone who is or was recently amongst the wolves. You will need the ability to be a good soldier, meaning able to endure much to give yourself a pat on the back and encourage yourself. It takes time for those amongst and recently from amongst the wolves to see what you see. Many of them have been blinded and lost from the exposure of reality and acceptance of truth. When we are dealing with our loved ones in this state, we want them to know what we know. We want them to understand and see the main point, but we cannot force them to see what we already see and they do not. We cannot force them to understand what we understand and they do not.

When someone has been influenced by wolves, they must come to themselves on their own. In my words, "coming to self" is to form decisions on disputed, controversial or doubtful matters, to realize the need for change, then to make action toward bringing the needed change to reality. You can set your loved one back many years by opening up your mouth at the wrong time. You can cause people who are already on the edge to have a major setback or, more seriously, even commit suicide; they are already on the edge. Be quiet when it's time to be silent. You can promote danger for them instead of help by not being a good soldier; you can push them from having a chance to survive to little or none at all. We must let God do his job; it's very important that we do not try to fix what only God can. You do not have to force people to come to themselves; just let God be God. I know it's hard to look at your loved one going through so much when there is nothing you can do but be still. It is okay to endure like a good soldier and be still and let God be God.

When you want to say something just silence yourself and talk to God about it. Surrender totally over to God. Be okay with God's way of doing things, not your way. You don't just tell a newborn baby to hurry up and walk; there is a process and it takes time. A baby has many delicate seasons where they can only be handled with care; there are some things we don't talk to babies about. We talk baby language in some seasons.

In some seasons you need to be quiet and don't offer your advice. Don't force them to get it, black mail or use manipulation for them to hurry up and get it. Don't handicap them by giving them whatever they want; don't be a doormat. We are to be as gentle as doves but as wise as serpents.

You must endure as a good soldier because you're going to have to encourage yourself. You're going to have to pat yourself on the back and tell yourself you are doing a good job. You're going to have to embrace yourself because someone that is among the wolves is not strong enough to support you nor take on negativity; they're in healing for themselves from negativity. You must endure for the sake of building them back up and to keep yourself built up. They are not your shoulder to cry on; you must be that for them.

It's dangerous for the hurt to lead the hurt. You must be strong, wise and gentle so you push them forward and not backwards. Don't set them backwards with wrong advice that causes them and others difficulty. You can avoid this by consulting God concerning the correct and helpful advice to give to them. You must endure so that they can heal healthily and recover in a healthy environment. Then they may obtain complete healing and grow with consistent progress. Endure so that they aren't set back nor thrown back to the wolves; they may not make it this time.

You know that you're on the right road to being a good soldier when you are not preaching to your loved one every day about the past with the "should have's and could have's" speeches and when you're not complaining. Instead you are praying about the things that hurt while in the process of supporting the loved one and helping them in the discovery of self and regaining of identity. You are not rushing and trying to make things happen; you are leaning to God's understanding and letting God be the lead, staying out of the way of the move of God, and letting God be the captain of you and them. You don't see yourself as better than them and you hold everything captive to God.

Remember: your loved one is the one that has to come to the realization of what you already see, what they probably should know by now but do not. You should have the wisdom, knowledge and understanding to help them gently overcome the challenges in the process of coming from amongst wolves. You are the one who has been set free; they are the ones that need to be lead to freedom. They are the ones who need the realization. They are the ones that need to come to themselves, and they do not need us to pressure them to realize truth.

This causes me to think about the story of the prodigal son in the bible, the part where he comes to himself and realization kicks in for him. His family was not around; he was off to himself. God knows how to get your loved one to "come to themselves" without the need of us pressuring them into doing so. There are some parts they must do while you only support by guiding them to the truth, but do not attempt to make them see the truth. This takes much patience so pull yourselves up and endure the process like a good soldier.

Enduring like a good soldier is a requirement in order to win them from the wolves and for the prevention of them returning to the wolves or losing them to just giving up. You complaining and whining will not be helpful to you, them or the process to freedom. Avoid causing anxiety or any kind of actions to make them see that you are right about what you are saying to them.

I know that you love them; your relationship will improve by providing support. This is not the place where you get points for being right or for celebrating that you were right all along. Rather it is a time that you realize the importance of your endurance in seeing this task through as a good soldier with the delicate wisdom, knowledge and understanding that is needed to help someone recover from hurt within improper relationships and regain their identity.

It is important that you understand one of the most powerful ministries that each one of us has is to minister the giving of love. Release your ministry of love, for love has the power to heal, clean, correct, restore and bring life to dead, stale areas which seem to be hopeless. I pray that you would really understand deeply the delicate position you are in, so I write this letter to you for the one that God has entrusted you to bring from amongst the wolves. We that are amongst the wolves would love to be able to say this to you. Please receive this as a letter from those amongst wolves. This is my belief of what that letter would say if they had all the words and the answers already to the transition from amongst wolves.

Dear entrusted loved one,

Thank you for assisting God in the task of bringing me from amongst the wolves. Please overlook my current behavior; I have been taught how to love from situations and circumstances where people held the characteristics of wolves. The wolves taught me to run and reject true love, so I cannot always recognize diamonds. My vision is unclear right now. Please love me not based on me being a drug dealer, on drugs, gossiper, or having sex out of wedlock; you know my unfinished flawed state.

Tell me that I am fearfully and wonderfully made, that I am a warrior. Tell me that I am a conqueror, that I have valor. Tell me that I am strong, not weak, so that I may become this. Tell me you adore me. Call me what you want me to become and speak to the finished state. It's taking much to get me to the finish line.

To be honest, I am afraid. Can you love me in the journey and not abandon me? I know I was in the crack house just last night and I am going today, or where ever that place is that isn't good for me. I still want love, confirmation, validation and approval. I need to be dealt with not from my current state, but from my finished state, where there are no blemishes, no stains and no wrinkles.

One amongst wolves deep down wants to say:
I am hurting, but the wolves taught me not to show it. They taught me to not let you in, telling me that you're going to hurt me again.

I need you to deal with me with my finished state in front of you, not my current.

Enduring like a soldier is a powerful stand that I ask you to take, although it will not be easy. Those that are amongst wolves are desperate for answers and healing, whether they will admit it or not.

THE PROCESS OF ENDURING
AS GOOD SOLDIERS

The process you will have to endure for your
loved one to not be lost to the wolves is a slow
process; it takes time for them to come from the
mindset they have been in so long. You must not
rush the process of transition to healing, the
work of God in all areas of their lives and
renewing of mindset and viewpoints. Rushing
the process and getting into your emotions can
bring about a setback in their process in
discovery of self, complete healing and recovery
in all areas of their lives. It can also bring about
a loss of trust to let you in their deepest
heartfelt moments of progress or to even ask
you for help. You may lose the honor of being in
a relationship with the person you desperately
need to bring from amongst wolves and give
support to not go back.

It is important in the process of being a good
soldier that you let them initiate what's right for
them. Do not insinuate nor makes hints or
suggestions in a sly manner to what you believe
to be right for them. This is a time when they
must acknowledge what is right for them and to
believe in themselves. They are learning to trust
their God-given instincts again. Let the time be
about them and their process of healing, not
yours.

47

In this process of enduring as a good soldier for your loved one, you can expect those amongst the wolves to be double minded. One minute they will say they will leave out of the bad relationship or situation, then the next minute they will find something to convince themselves it's their God-given purpose to stay in this unhealthy situation and/or relationship. The enemy has attempted to pervert their intelligence and twist their identity and truth of who God really is; some have come into a belief system that God is going to punish them if they leave the situation.

It's sad that they've been so long with the wolves that they sense there's something wrong, but their sense to respond to their instinct is watered out to nearly nothing. They are drained; the strategy of the wolves is to always keep them drained, hopeless, restless, broken, and not believing in themselves. To keep them from walking into purpose is the main reason, the very reason of the counteraction.

The enemy Satan's objective is to keep your loved one receiving the counterfeit; Satan's mission uses the wolves to trap a person in, tangle them, twist and pervert their mind, emotions and intelligence. The enemy knows how much ground he loses when a person discovers purpose and begins to walk in their purpose, so Satan's strategy with those amongst wolves is to keep them far away from learning anything about their God-given purpose. The game plan is to keep your loved one from discovery of destiny, to cause them to not see purpose clearly. He sends all kinds of distraction to keep them blinded and in chains and behind bars, where they're their own jailer with the keys in their own hands. The enemy knows he doesn't have to steal the keys to freedom, just their mind. The enemy knows that if he gets a person's mind he can control their body, life, movement and every decision they make. This is why the double-minded spirit is so very high in operation; the enemy coils his lies around your loved one's mind.

For those that are the ones amongst the wolves, you must renew your mind. It is the desire of the enemy to prevent you from seeing things clearly, to cause you to not react correctly or in a manner that leads to truth. The enemy also knows he doesn't have to take truth from you; he only needs to twist it, using what you care about to twist the truth, to mess with your perception of the truth. Even when truth is in front of you, you can see it but cannot perceive it correctly.

You must pray for your loved ones not only to get the truth but to perceive it correctly and have no part of the truth be distorted. You must pray they operate in a sound mind, getting cleansing and daily washing and renewing of the mind for your loved one. Pray that they perceive truth correctly and untwisted, that they love the truth and hate lies to such a degree that they stay open for the truth only and walk in it all the days of their life. Pray against pride and shame. Pray to bind the cunning craftsmanship of the wolves at work with Satan as their leader.

You must pray all kinds of prayers in all kinds of areas, but not aimlessly. That is why I am writing this book, to reveal to you the areas and the strategies of how to pray without shooting aimlessly and missing the very areas needing your attention. To avoid wasting time while in prayer, follow God's guidance on what to pray for the person.

You must be careful not to rush your loved one through the recovery process; rushing can cause them to run back amongst wolves. You must be wise as a serpent, gentle as a dove and ready at a moment's notice to celebrate even the smallest truth. Celebrating the truth helps them to welcome more truth.

Remember that almost every day amongst the wolves is a state of misery - no matter how big the smile on their face is in public. True love needs to be demonstrated so that they know the differences between improper love and proper love. In the world we live in, there are many who have never seen true love demonstrated in their homes. It is important to give them the truth by providing them with the demonstration of true love.

In the process of enduring as a good soldier, you can become frustrated while dealing with the mindset of those who have been recently or who currently are amongst the wolves. They can be hard to get through to at times because you think differently from them in some areas. The healing process can be intense, but you can decide not to let frustration cause you to lose your gentleness.

You will need your gentleness in this process. Once gentleness is lost, many begin to speak out of emotions, speaking things that are not true, and some even begin to call them what the wolves and others are saying that are not what God says about them. Instead of saying things that are not helpful, tell them who God says they are. Help them to seek God to reveal more of who they are; that is what they are missing. They can sense that they are not a wolf, that it is not a good situation, but they are lost; identity must be regained each time.

Tell them, *you are strong and you will survive,* and tell and show them what they will never be told and shown amongst the wolves. This gives them strength. This enhances their fighting ability. It gives the strength needed to fight when necessary instead of withdrawal from fighting. Speak uplifting words which replenish them with courage to continue to fight for freedom. Never speak negatively, but always speak to them about who they are and their purpose. Speak of how much God loves them.

Fill them with as much biblical word as possible, even if you have to tell it in parables. They don't have to know it's bible; some are taught by wolves not to be speaking that Jesus stuff. You can say, *I know of this man named David who took down a giant with a rock and his belief; all things are possible with God*. Remember: we must be as wise as serpents and as gentle as doves.

Allowing those currently amongst wolves to decide on their own to leave the wolves avoids you being blamed for everything that doesn't go right. Remember in the bible the Hebrews Moses led out of slavery blamed him for things that were not his fault, complaining to him about all kinds of things. Just as the Hebrews in the bible still thought as slaves although they were free, those that have been recently amongst the wolves think as if they are still amongst the wolves.

Only put faith in that which God releases to you. You want to put faith in what God is in agreement with. Sometimes living amongst wolves brings a way of thinking that causes one to apply faith amiss. Their minds are twisted and coiled in disbelief and untruthfulness. The environment amongst wolves is one that has no truth or healing. They have no support amongst wolves; they are daily prey. The wolves want them hopeless and operating in a broken spirit with broken dreams.

You see, being amongst wolves teaches them how to paint and show off picture perfect. In public they will wave and smile at people with the intentions of convincing them all is good and that they're happy while hurting deeply on the inside. They fake happiness and unity; they apply makeup to cover the bruises and wounds in all areas, not just physically. Amongst wolves, wounds get covered up and issues get bigger instead of dealt with.

These unhealthy relationships force your loved ones to hold inside even the deepest concerns. Many amongst the wolves stick up for the wolves; remember that wolves go in packs and stick together. Those amongst wolves pick up the manner to protect the wolves. Some of your loved ones are willing to give up their lives, dreams and goals to protect the wolves.

This reminds me of Ananias and Sapphira in Acts 5: 1-11 (KJV). Sapphira told a lie with her husband Ananias.

> [1]But a certain man named Ananias, with Sapphira his wife, sold a possession, [2]And kept back *part* of the price, his wife also being privy *to it*, and brought a certain part, and laid *it* at the apostles' feet. [3]But Peter said, Ananias, why hath Satan filled thine heart to lie to the Holy Ghost, and to keep back *part* of the price of the land?
>
> [4]Whiles it remained, was it not thine own? and after it was sold, was it not in thine own power? why hast thou conceived this thing in thine heart? thou hast not lied unto men, but unto God. [5]And Ananias hearing these words fell down, and gave up the ghost: and great fear came on all them that heard these things. [6]And the young men arose, wound him up, and carried *him* out, and buried *him*.
>
> [7]And it was about the space of three hours after, when his wife, not knowing what was done, came in. [8]And Peter answered unto her, Tell me whether ye sold the land for so much? And she said, Yea, for so much. [9]Then Peter said unto her, How is it that ye have agreed together to tempt the Spirit of the Lord? behold, the feet of them

which have buried thy husband *are* at the door, and shall carry thee out. [10]Then fell she down straightway at his feet, and yielded up the ghost: and the young men came in, and found her dead, and, carrying *her* forth, buried *her* by her husband. [11]And great fear came upon all the church, and upon as many as heard these things.

Many will lie for the wolves to cover up truth and to protect the wolves at all costs although it's clearly not commendable. Your loved one has been taught how to love self improperly because they have been loved improperly. They see lying as protection to wolves, as keeping peace and showing their love and dedication.

Real love welcomes and shows appreciation for you telling the truth, and you are handled gently for telling the truth. Amongst the wolves, you're not in an environment that welcomes truth. Truth is like breaking the highest law amongst wolves because truth brings freedom and wolves hates it; the wolves do not want your loved one free ever.

PART 2: THE STAGES AMONGST WOLVES

WHY IT IS IMPORTANT
TO KNOW THE DIFFERENT STAGES

Each stage or season must be dealt with in wisdom, not just in any kind of manner. There's a stage when you must speak and then there is a stage when you must be quiet, when it is not for you to speak.

During the early stages of having a loved one amongst wolves, there's much distortion of truth in the process and the loved one is often unaware. They are becoming more and more blinded to the truth. I urge you to be quiet in this season and frequently seek the Lord. Listen and watch more than you speak; most of the time speaking out what you believe at this time is not a good move. In the beginning stages your loved one does not realize that they are amongst wolves, and if you open your mouth too soon they will see you as a wolf instead of seeing the actual wolf. You must go to the Father and ask Him for the strategy; do not proceed with leaning to your own understanding.

In the middle stages of being amongst wolves, your loved one's thinking is perverted deeply. It's like a done deal in the decision of them wanting the wolf to be in and a part of every area of their life. You cannot walk up to your loved one and tell them the person is clearly a wolf. You must be as wise as a serpent but gentle as a dove; challenge them to ask questions and look a little closer, to really take thought. Challenge them to think things through and pray.

Most of the time your loved one in this stage doesn't understand why you do not see the goodness in the person that is a wolf, as they do. They begin to think you're just a hater or don't want to see goodness for them when you open your mouth too soon. This is why in this stage it is important to be quiet, although it may be tough. You need the relationship to be open in order to help them. Remember that their sight is blinded and twisted to truth at this stage.

Pray against the spirit of deception. This is a stage where you should seek the Lord's counsel and direction. Show no reactions of the dislike and don't try to show that you want them apart from the wolf. Most of the time your loved one will draw closer to the wolf and find a way to shut you out completely, or the wolves will come with major strategy and brainwashing of your loved one's thoughts; they will bring about actions to drown you out as the influence of your loved one's life. You must not show your hatred. The wolves target those that can smell or see them as a direct enemy that needs to be dealt with to prevent their plans from failing.

This is why Little Red Riding Hood's Grandmother was put in the closet, so she would not be able to interfere with the wolf taking the granddaughter's goods (and God knows what else). The grandmother was tied up to hinder movement and exposure of the wolf's plans. In the same way, your loved one's wolf may have these intentions toward you when you expose yourself.

You must keep quiet in that season. You must keep quiet in words and about what you know to be true. I say again: be wise as serpents and gentle as doves. Collect information and instead of talking, listen. Tell God everything and ask Him to fix it and not you. Talking to God gives you peace to keep on, to keep on without losing yourself in your emotions.

Not being aware of the stage your loved one is in can cause harm that could have been prevented had you dealt with the situation in wisdom. Spend much time asking God what season your loved one is in and what strategy is to be used. It is important to know the different stages because it plays a big part in freedom and prevention of unnecessary setbacks. It helps you to not shoot aimlessly in this spiritual warfare. In no stage should you become anxious; instead pray without ceasing and without getting into your emotions. Speaking with divine wisdom prevents unnecessary struggles and the need for many detours and delays.

Hold what you do and plan to do, captive to God. Ask him, *shall I do this*? This is one of the reasons that David in the bible was so successful in subduing his enemies. What I like about David is him inquiring to God about his enemies caused him to receive new strategies and insights. It's a terrible thing to not inquire of the Lord when He knows everything and to instead just assume that the last instruction He gave you would be okay to use again because you are fighting the same enemy. I encourage new strategy and insight each time.

Ask God, *shall I have this discussion? Is the time right to have this discussion? What tone should I use? How, when, and in what matter shall I do this or that? What do you want me to do and how do you want me to do it?* Ask the Lord, *when, where, and God what shall be my attitude?* I have learned that God is not afraid to give details; we are sometimes too afraid to ask Him for the details in our lives. Ask for God's protection for you and others that may be involved directly or indirectly.

There are some stages when you must speak, but you must know when. In this season it can hurt your loved one for you not to speak truth in love and cause you to be in regret that you did not speak. When God says speak, have no fear. Speak.

There is even a stage when you must withdraw, when it is too dangerous for you even to be seen or involved at this time. Your assignment is to love them at a distance, praying for them on situations when they are not strong enough or able to at the moment.

There are other stages when you must speak goodness into their life by making decrees and declarations concerning them. This helps to build confidence. You must challenge them to speak no negativity.

In other stages you must pray for yourself to not be fooled by the enemy. This is the blend in stage because in this stage it can seem as if you have already lost to the enemy, but the devil is a liar. A sheep can pretend to be a wolf only for so long. What is inside of you must come out sooner or later.

There is a stage when your loved one must prepare to leave. For the one amongst the wolves in the stage of preparing to leave, it is important you remain normal, as if nothing is changing. You must more than any other time be wise but gentle as a dove, showing no aggression or fed up attitude for the wolves to pick up on. This helps you to leave in peace.

Before you leave, signs that you plan to leave can cause unnecessary fighting and physical assaults when the wolves react in rage. Do not run to the wolves to seek approval for what you are doing. I know you have been around the wolves for so long that you still want to share things with them to see if they will care, to see if they will make any last minute changes. I caution you: this is dangerous. To be honest with you, the wolves only care about themselves. They will use every piece of information you leak out to them to protect themselves and devour by all means. I would like to save you unnecessary trouble and hardship.

Keep your mouth closed about your moves of leaving. This even helps those with children and others that God has sent to help you be protected from unseen damages and hardship in the process of you leaving. Do not be self-centered in this time and forget to think about others attached to you. I have heard of wolves killing family members to prevent them from helping someone leave because they had to tell the wolves every plan they came up with.

For some of you amongst wolves, because of how violent wolves can become about your freedom, be quiet about your movement in leaving until the last minute. For some that includes those close to you. Many may not be able to tell family members nor their children until after, and even then let God tell you what you share. The wolves are clever to use those that you told against you, unknown to those whose real intention was to help you. The bible says, *do not let the right hand know what the left hand knows.* Not telling the wolves your plans to relocate or get from amongst them will help you avoid having your plans intercepted by the enemy, hindrance and delays in progress to freedom and taking on more pressure than necessary.

If the loved one is coming to live with you or moving near you, whomever you are going to help come from amongst the wolves, you must prepare your heart, mind and emotions to be tough and to also have great hospitality. Make the living situation comfortable the best you can.

Understand that the loved one sometimes will think about going back amongst the wolves. This is a stage, just as the Hebrew people Moses led out of Egypt in the bible asked God to be free. They got the courage to leave, but along the journey they became overtaken in this transition period from a slave to no more a slave. They began to complain and ask to go back into slavery, thinking it would be better rather than to get accustomed to all the newness (Numbers 14:2-4). You see, although they were free, they still thought like slaves. That caused things to be a struggle as they attempted to apply old methods in the new. They became frustrated because at this stage, many thought, *at least we knew how to do for ourselves in the old* (although it was hard and tough).

In their freedom, there's no more depending on their strength, knowledge or ability; now it's totally trusting God and relying upon Him for everything. Many times, you must operate in blind faith and the instructions are not released until you complete the last thing already instructed. This is so new to them that they become weary, thinking they are nothing because what used to work does not work here. They begin to think they should go back to the familiar, but this is the place that God has desired them to come into from the very beginning.

Pray against false burdens for your loved one in this season. They are dealing with much at this time, many concerns they are ashamed to speak of to anyone. Be a friend. If you are mom, be a friend more than a parent and develop a relationship. Ask what they like; don't just assume they like what they once did in past times. Challenge them to search out who they are; gently, not forcefully, they must discover their identity and heal. This is very important because it develops the character that will cause them to not go back or attach to wolves.

THE BEGINNING STAGE

You walk into the wolves. They talk and show pretty picture shows at this season; they lure you in. The wolves are doing lots of deception and planning at this stage. Everything is a lie. There is only enough truth told to deceive you. This process can go on for some time. At this time the wolves are consistently moving in for the right time. Each time, the wolves target at breaking you of your strength.

At this stage, stay watchful and keep an eye on the loved one you are helping to come from amongst the wolves. Here the wolves are coming up with plots to get your loved one away from any possible good influence, or just talking your loved one against you. They want to cause your loved one to think that those that love them aren't creditable of being trusted for telling the truth.

The wolves want us to begin to say and see truth as a lie at this stage and they will go as far as pretending that the truth is wrong, just to play mind manipulation games. But one of their many objectives is to get rid of those that love you, care for you and stand for you. The wolves desire to destroy those that reveal them, especially those that see them well.

To those that have loved ones at this stage, please don't allow the wolf to notice that you know they are wolves, and don't tell your loved one that you know. Your loved one at this stage is so twisted that they would repeat every word you have said to the wolves and take side with the wolves. Your loved one must see that the person, situation or circumstance is a wolf for themselves.

In your conversations with your loved one in this stage, listen to why they see what they see in the wolf and challenge them to search out details more carefully and think through the detail more strictly. This is what causes Little Red Riding Hood to see more clearly. Once Little Red Riding Hood started to look at the details, she began to ask questions that caused the wolf to become uncomfortable.

Asking questions focused on their identity brings discomfort; it causes wolves to expose themselves more quickly and to lose courage or thrill in pursuing. Little Red Riding Hood began to ask question that caused the wolf to be uncomfortable, saying "what big eyes you have and what big teeth you have."

The wolf does not want your loved one to think at this stage. They want to make your loved one feel safe and like they are the best thing that could possibly ever happen in their life at this timing, like they are the only ones that understand what they are going through.

The wolf at this stage tells them good things. Whenever they are wrong, they don't tell them; they do not care. If they are right, they still don't care. Wrong or right, they do not make them feel uncomfortable. They attempt to make them feel loved and accepted in their right and wrong moments. So you cannot approach your loved one talking about they're wrong for staying out with the married man, or for swinging on the pole all night.

Trust me...the wolves celebrate with them for this and give them rewards of special treatment. Which do you think a person in this situation wants: the special treatment, extra loving attention or the rebuke? I would take the special treatment. I wouldn't want all that: *you going to hell, God going to get you*. You must use strategy that God gives you in this stage.

THE CONVINCING STAGE

This is where the wolves convince them that they are the only ones that really care for them. The breaking of self-esteem sometimes happens in this stage. The wolves have convinced your loved one that it is okay not to have those who support and love them around anymore. The convincing stage is where the stripping of their identity is starting, and most of the time they are deeply in love with the wolves at this stage.

To those amongst the wolves, it is here that little by little you are degraded for what you have done. The wolf is no longer giving you praise for the right things; that was just in the beginning stage. You are made to feel like you only have worth and value with them. You struggle with who you are; who you are is being drowned to the point of you not knowing.

You no longer have standards. You should, but the wolves take you through the convincing stage just to get you confused. You are so confused about who you are. You are so confused that you try to blend in and do what the wolves do, thinking maybe you are a wolf too. You say stuff like, *I can do that also*, although it never feels right. You want to believe and not believe what those who really love you say. You don't want to let them down.

You don't know what the outcome of your life will be. You should have goals that support you for the years ahead. They should be positive for you, plans that lead to freedom.

It is at this stage that you are confused and you need someone to tell you who you are. The wolves never tell you the truth; they love that you are confused. They can run over you easier when you are confused. *Maybe*, is what you say often. *Maybe I will do that. I am not sure. I do not know.* And you really don't. You rely on the wolves to get approval on when and how to make the smallest decisions. You must stop this.

You can do things without them being with you; you are not handicapped. You are worth more than the wolves tell you. You are not worthless. In fact, that is the very reason the wolves want to keep you in bondage, because of the threat you are to their wolf pack and their master. You *are* someone. You will regain your stand again. You will come to the terms where anything does not go. You don't have to live your life with small and great things being dictated step for step, having no say-so or support on any good ideas. You have say-so.

I challenge you to begin to command your morning as God urged Job in the bible to do. You must begin to speak highly of yourself. Agree with what God says about you (Psalm 139:14):

you are fearfully and wonderfully made and you can do all things through Christ who strengthens you. Depend on, trust and run to God for everything. Let God direct your steps and stop doing things your way. Do it God's way. God wants you to have goodness.

In the bible, the Lord says to Jeremiah in KJV Jeremiah 29:11:

> *For I know the plans I have for you, saith the LORD, thoughts of peace, and not of evil, to give you an expected end.*

THE REASONING STAGE

Here you are trying to say you have a good reason for staying amongst the wolves.

When you submit to God's perfect will and settle for nothing less, God gives you His perfect will in all areas of your life, even in your relationships. He guides you to what is good for you. Some just want God's permissive will and God will give you what you desire. In the bible, God tells us life and death stand before us. Then He says choose life. He is telling us which is best for us, telling us which way we should go, but He will not force us. In the same way, in all areas of your life, God will lead you in the way you should go. He has already gone before us and prepared the way we should go, but He will not force us to take the way He has prepared.

God gives us free will and choice. The truth is that many have chosen what they wanted and put God on it. You got into it yourself and convinced yourself that God was happy and pleased with you for doing so. You feel like God should be happy with what you have done and you have convinced yourself that God is happy. You are suffering in this relationship, using misapplied terms to justify applying faith amiss. You make remarks such as, "*nobody told us the road would be easy*," with the intention of using these terms to encourage yourself to continue to remain in unhealthiness. This is the spirit of deception at the greatest level of deception.

Many people spend much time in dead relationships. It is very important not to handle dead things. It's a great task to make and convince yourself every day that someone loves you. You have to think up the things of the past that justify that they love you. That's not really love, but you can start loving yourself today.

The truth is that you are in deep fear. The spirit of deception works in fear. You see things that are not present, afraid to leave a bad situation. You are tolerating bad situations because you don't feel like you're going to have better, and then turn around blaming God with a mindset that you are doing God a favor. You think you're being obedient to God when you're being rebellious to God's will and purpose of your life. God is not calling you to stay stuck all your life. Believe me, that is not the purpose of your life.

The truth of the matter is that you are free to leave first base and even after making it and skidding on to second base, you want to run back to first base all because second base is too far away from the familiar. I challenge you to come out of fear. Stop looking at shadows as if they are real. Believe in yourself and rely on God.

THE LOSING ALL GROUNDS STAGE

The wolves want your loved one to know that there's no reason for them to think. This is the mindset they attempt to create, to stop your loved one from thinking for themselves and instead to leave thinking unto the wolves. The very reason is to cause your loved one to lose confidence in trusting themselves, which causes them to not listen to their God-given instincts. Instead of listening to their God-given instincts, they now come to the wolves to ask for permission to do simple things.

That is exactly what the wolves want: to know your loved one's exact moves for the purpose of hindering them from discovering their identity. The wolves want them under control; your loved one has lost their voice and their stand. Most of all, if not bad enough already, they no longer really know what they stand for any more. They have not stood for what they truly desired, or knew what they wanted. And since it's been that they have not stood for themselves, they are afraid to do so at all. Losing their identity follows in this stage.

In this stage, you must remind them of who they are; they really do not know. They are blind and the spirit of deception is operating. They protect the wolves at all costs. They are exhausted with even the idea of fighting. They have accepted that this is just their life. They have accepted that happiness is for others but not for them - that it is just their life to not be happy.

Their discerning is low; they believe whatever the wolves say most of the time. Even when the lie is clear in their face, they cannot see it clearly. The deception is strong. The lies are so deep. The entanglement of the wolves' grip is strong, like a consistent rope around their neck, daring them to do or say anything wrong such as attempt to get free or stand up for themselves. That was one of the plots of the wolves: to cause the person amongst the wolves to lose their stand. When one gives up their stand, they stop fighting and dismiss their dreams.

To the loved one of those amongst the wolves, please challenge them to believe in themselves again. Remind them of who they are at the right time, the time that matters the most. Do so wisely without over-exaggerating. Speak to them and remind them of the warrior in them. Remind them of what they used to not take. Remind them of things that are sure to remind them of the courage they took in fearful situations.

Speak good things to them. Do not remind them of the wrong or of what they should have not done. Secretly, they now know that they are not in a good situation. They know that they are not properly loved, but they do not know how to get out. This is the stage when they're tired of fighting. They think they can't leave. They wonder how they're supposed to leave.

THE GLUED STAGE

You're so stuck. You make up situations and circumstances that are not there, saying you will leave when this or that happens. *I cannot leave now because I have to have this happen first*, when those things that you use as excuses to delay leaving are not even real situations that are preventing you from leaving at all. You must get real with yourself.

Separate the lies from the truth, what is real and what isn't. I know when you're amongst wolves you learn to act and pretend things are good when they are not and give up on dreams. It seems good to stop reaching for dreams because they seem to never come anyway. I am so sad for you right now; this has got to stop. You have got to come out of this glued mindset way of thinking that there's no way out or that it's too much or impossible.

You've got to ask for help. You've got to use your voice. You keep seeking help. I don't care who didn't help you last time or what the outcome was the last time; you seek out help. You've got to keep knocking on doors. You've got to get out. I know it's hard to see yourself free or able to be free, but see yourself free anyway.

Pray for your loved one in this stage consistently, for truth and most of all for God to bind deception and everything the enemy attempts to use to cause blockages from seeing and receiving the truth. I pray that your loved one would get their fight back and dismiss every excuse and lie. I pray that they will put into action every idea God has given them and take action of the ideas as God expects them to. I pray for them to be courageous in this season, not tired or weary.

I pray they know they can win, they can make it and they can overcome if they just believe and take their power back from the enemy. I pray that they believe that they really can do all things through Christ who strengthens us. I pray they take their power back and pick up the sword of God and use it very wisely. I pray they will surrender to God and allow God to deal with their unbelief.

THE "I WANT OUT" STAGE

This is the stage when you just know you want out. Exhaustion can no longer be ignored and you become aware of how the improper relationship has put stress on you physically, mentally, financially, spiritually, emotionally, and socially. You become aware of how others are being affected in their growth due to being attached to you while you deal with improper relationships. You are tired of the replay, the same old same old.

It's at this point when you are just like whatever, there's not even enough strength given from the relationship to even fight for it. You know for sure you really want out. You are to the point you say it every now and then and are content with picturing life apart from the wolves. You begin to see yourself for who you are. It is here in this stage that you become more open to healing and the possibility of having more than the current. This is the stage when you are becoming more truthful with yourself and others than ever before. I encourage you to continue in the truth, for it is the truth that sets us free.

For those with a loved one amongst wolves, it is here when your loved one can see themselves out of their current situation. Freedom is starting to happen in the inside. Freedom happens on the inside first, then in the natural. Continue to pray that they let God walk out healing on the inside of them and that they remain open to His moving in all areas of their lives. They are coming out.

THE BLEND IN STAGE

The blend in stage comes before survival. This is where we are off balance. It is at this stage that we are confused about who we are and burdened with many unanswered questions. The enemy has used much rejection to get us here - not just rejection from the wolves, but also from having loved ones who do not understand what it's like to be amongst wolves nor how the association with wolves teaches you to love.

It is here where we don't fit in many places, are looked down on, and experience the most rejection by our loved ones and the wolves. So in order to not be rejected by the wolves we blend. This is where we appear to be like those we are amongst and even as those that we are not like. We are in a battle for our lives and blending in is a way to survive.

It is here where we are in need of the most prayers and expressions of love. We are becoming comfortable with being tougher than tough; this is the only reaction that seems to stop others from breaking us. Silence becomes our greatest enemy and friend; as sad as this is, more often than not our old friends or our family don't want us because they do not understand us. It makes our situation more perplexed when we have to defend ourselves both amongst the wolves and our loved ones consistently. Yet still our loved ones, and those God has entrusted to protect us, do not understand that we are at the mercy of the wolves. We've learned to think like, act like and correspond to the liking of the wolves. We've learned to adjust to the environment, in which wolves live in order to survive, or else the wolves would have killed us or we would have killed ourselves.

When you are not a wolf yourself and you must lie amongst wolves, you have to function in a certain way to not be killed. Some of you need to forgive your kids and even your spouses or other family members. Someone who was not a crackhead had to look like one. Someone who was not a prostitute had to blend in, because amongst the wolves either you do what a prostitute does or look like one in order to survive.

The bible says we are fearfully and wonderfully made. It doesn't say we *will be* fearfully and wonderfully made; it said we already were made this way *Psalms 139:14*. So now you're looking like something you are not.

One may say that it's horrible that you would have to do that, to look like something you are not. They'd say that you should just come from amongst the wolves. When you're amongst wolves it doesn't work like that. I read an article online entitled, Getting Out Alive: Wolf Attack (http://wilderness-urban-survival.blogspot.com/2010/02/wolf-attack.html?m=1). The article listed thirteen actions to protect yourself in an encounter with wolves.

1. Up a tree — that's not a bad idea. Wolves can't climb trees, so you are safe if you can get up one. However, the wolf (or the pack) might just take up residence at the base of the tree and wait for you to get tired and come down.

2. Maintain a clean camp to keep from attracting wolves into camp with the smell of food.

3. Don't run, as that will only stimulate the wolf to attack. You can't outrun them, so you have to stand and fight for your life.

4. Try to make yourself look as large as possible. Wave your arms and coat, hoist a backpack overhead to make you look bigger.

5. Do not make eye contact, because that is taken as an act of aggression on your part and might trigger an attack.

6. Don't grin or show your teeth, for the same reason.

7. Get on your feet and kick, scream and fight back. Wolves have been known to attack humans as they slept in sleeping

bags, where the victim is at a serious disadvantage. The sooner you can get up on your feet and start yelling at the wolf and fighting back, the better.

8. Use any weapon at hand, a club, a walking staff, a knife, a gun, a mountaineering axe.
9. Try to strike its nose, as this is a very sensitive area.
10. Protect your face and throat by using your forearm to fend off the attack.
11. As last resort, ram your fist down the animal's throat. You will get torn up a bit, but the wolf won't be able to rip up more critical parts of your body.
12. Stay in groups. Wolves are less likely to attack if you are in a large group than if you are alone.
13. Maintain a fire in camp all night, because wolves don't like fire.

You must use strategy for survival; you can't just leave as people say. People in gangs can't just leave and live to tell the story.

I speak to those that have family members, friends and even those you have not met yet that have been taught how to love from being in the environment and presence of wolves. I caution you from just giving your loved one advice on how to come from amongst wolves. Most of the time we who are amongst wolves are given the advice from loved ones to just leave; that will get you killed. Our family members seem to become resentful toward us for not taking their advice to just get up and leave, as if it were good advice.

In the blend in stage, many lose their loved ones, reject them and abandon them. Many want nothing to do with their loved ones in this stage; they feel that they have lost the fight in winning them. God says that is not so; the wolves are using strategy and He wants you to use strategy to win your loved one from amongst the wolves. God wants you to seek Him for the answers and the strategies to help them come from the thinking they've developed while living amongst wolves; He wants you to use these strategies without damaging them further. Those that are amongst the wolves are precious to God. God loves them very much and His glory is embedded on the inside of them.

God no longer wants us to shoot aimlessly in winning our loved ones. Winning has to be done with the proper strategies and the right timing for using the strategies that God gives you. God says ask and it shall be given. Do not think that because of how bad it looks that God cannot save your loved one. Trust God for the strategy that is needed for the person. Each person is dealing with a different wolf or wolves and a different strategy is needed.

Always consult God before doing anything and do not assume the strategy he gave you prior is the one He wants you to use each time or ever again. Keep going to God for the correct strategy to use at each time and always ask for the correct timing to use it. You can do it. In the blend in stage, your loved one most often needs your meekness, not your toughness.

THE SURVIVAL STAGE

In this stage, you are just trying to survive. Your thinking becomes survival. In this stage, you start to realize the effects of being taught by wolves. You start to use what you have learned amongst the wolves to survive. You do what you have to do to survive.

To those with a loved one amongst the wolves, you see this as negative sometimes, saying that the person doesn't act the same anymore. Please recognize that they are in survival mode. They are getting tired of just letting everything go the wolves' way. They got tougher. Being taught how to love by wolves teaches you to be tough. In my opinion, it's part of surviving if you want to make it back alive. The problem is that many still are in survival mode when it's no longer needed anymore. You have to help the loved one through this.

Many times, those amongst the wolves are judged very harshly because people fail to realize what is happening and what has happened. They may be seen as horrible or bad, but if the toughness didn't come out, the wolves more than likely would have had their final desire, to cause even more damage. The survival stage is a sure sign your loved one is in a great fight. They need help, but do not expect them to come asking normally. Amongst wolves, letting people know you're in need causes the wolves to do hurtful and painful things toward your loved one. We are taught to be tough in order to survive from being in survival mode, to keep from being bullied and being pushed around. We are tired.

Amongst wolves, you learn not to let weakness show. You have to be tough, so you hide pain with anger, hurt with laughter, and tears are expression of happiness more than smiles. Smiles express disappointment.

You learn to not directly ask for help. You learn to ask in silence. You ask for help by complaining. In toughness, you learn to talk in circles because you don't know who to trust. You don't tell all; you tell bits and pieces due to lack of trust because you see you should not have trusted the wolves but yet you did. You no longer know who to really trust anymore. You are very cautious now, even when there isn't danger near.

Asking for help can get you hurt, killed, bullied, laughed at, or your confidence broken amongst wolves. You asking for help is boldness to the wolves that can cause freedom. The wolves know one of the quickest ways to come out of bondage is to ask for help from the right person or source. So here they break your confidence by trying to feed you lies, saying a thing like, that's *stupid, you know they're not going to help you*, or they call great ideas and truthful statements stupid. Well, you know this. The wolves do this strategy to keep you confused. That's why you must keep asking people for help.

For those with a loved one amongst wolves, especially amongst those that don't understand their situation, you can help the wolves out by passing judgments on your loved ones and not understanding those amongst wolves. Running to someone who doesn't understand is as hurtful as being amongst the wolves. The last thing needed is you to tell them what they can't do. They have gotten enough of being told what they could not do. Encourage and don't degrade them. Please love them. Your love ushers them into freedom quicker without a fight. They are already tired and exhausted in many areas.

PART 3: THE STAGES TO FREEDOM

REALIZATION

There are different processes which take place in freedom. One that's extremely important is to come into realization of truth. Any time we are dealing with freedom, you cannot leave truth out. The truth sets us free. The truth must start with you. You must be truthful with yourself. It is the key to freedom. Truth opens doors, causes you to see and hear clearly. It isn't always easy to be truthful. It takes courage and boldness. The truth begins to tear down lies and even separate lies from truth.

Lies keep us involved with wolves and unhealthy relationships. Lies hurt badly.

We must ask God for His help to lead us to truth. The truth is that we can be blinded to the truth. We cannot see it, receive it, or comprehend it; we can be, lost to the truth. We need God to really help us, to lead us to truth, to help see the truth and walk into the freedom the truth brings. It is very important that once God shows you truth you walk in the truth, living in the freedom the truth has brought you into and not returning to that which bounded you. Many get the truth; even more do not receive or hold to the truth. Don't reject the truth. Lean not to your own understanding, but instead seek God.

Coming fully into the truth causes you to walk into the truth and not forsake it for any reason. Many are able to discover truth, but few can receive it and walk in the truth. Pray that you accept and walk fully in the truth.

ACCEPTANCE

Your loved one must accept that until they come into acceptance of the truth they will not see clearly. I know sometimes we really want them to receive the truth and walk in it. It is very important that they not only obtain the truth, but receive it and also walk in it.

For those amongst wolves or who are on your way to freedom, you must accept the truth once it is revealed. Grab the truth and the freedom the truth provides. Don't give up your truth for nothing. Accept all of the truth; don't live in pride. Pride blocks us from accepting what causes forward progress. Pride brings destruction. Don't reject the truth; instead, accept truth and learn and grow from it. Don't behave as if something strange has happened to you. We fall down. Now get back up!

A sure sign one has come to true acceptance is not seeking anyone to blame and not making any excuses. At this point it is not about blaming or seeking whose fault it is. How you got here is not your focus. Put your focus on healing; focus on all the things that will bring true healing. Begin to accept and embrace reality without shame. Accept the situation or circumstance for what it truly is - not what you wanted yourself to believe, but truth. Reject all the lies you told

101

yourself (so many that you almost cannot separate what is real and what is not). I plead with you here. There is a major healing that leads you to a great amount of the freedom needed to move forward, and it is acceptance. You are no longer held captive or blaming yourself or others. Once you accept things for what they are, you are able to embrace truth with contentment and be okay with moving on. Just know that it is okay.

Yes, there will be pain in acceptance of the truth, but keep moving. This is good hurt because it brings healing and causes you to be loosed from the old hurt and lies which the wolves enjoyed telling you to prevent you from moving forward. I ensure you that the power you take back by acceptance of truth and rejection of lies will lead to great freedom.

Yes, you may have to admit you were in love with someone who never loved you. You may need help in many areas. You may have to accept many different things, but acceptance of them brings healing. You're coming out. The power of acceptance is so empowering that this alone gains you so much freedom. No longer can others or self pound you with the old hurt. No longer will you accept lies.

It is at this stage when you begin to take laughter back and reject living in shame. You take a stand again and are able to say *yes, I've done some stupid things but you or no one else can use them to hurt me or keep me in bondage.* Step out from shame, hurt, humiliation or whatever with your head held high. You are not the old person. You are walking out, no longer held captive by yourself or others. Here you learn how to say *yes, I did that and I'm not happy that I did it but I wear no shame. I have forgiven myself.*

You know that you have come into acceptance of the truth when you forgive yourself and all those who wronged you, those who attempted to wrong you and those that desire to. There's no anger when it's brought up by others, no resentment, no *I wish I would have done this.* Your mindset is more like, *this is the way I did it and I learned how to prevent getting into the same predicament.* Acceptance must continue to be done in other stages of your freedom.

DOUBT AND FEAR

Doubt and fear must go. I want to share my favorite bible verse and two others that helped me on my journey as I divorced doubt and fear. I kicked them all the way back to the pit of hell from which they had come. The enemy wanted to use the wolves to keep you here; it was a plot of the enemy Satan to keep you out of things that God had already ordained you to have. Some of those things are peace, joy and happiness. When you doubt, you are back and forth. Fear keeps you from doing what you know you must. Fear attempts to keep us from peace, joy and happiness.

> *2 Timothy 1:7 (KJV)*
> *For God hath not given us the spirit of fear; but of power, and of love, and of a sound mind.*

So the spirit of fear does not come from God. God does not want you in fear; God wants us to walk in faith, to believe and trust that all will be okay. Do not be afraid to walk away from all the things that have caused you to be stuck and not advance and all the people and associations that go along with it. Some amongst the wolves are even afraid of being alone, not being wanted by anyone else. The lies the enemies have told you are lies. Reject fear; do not allow fear to keep you stuck. Just choose to believe that God is able to restore your life, to put all the broken pieces back together again. You can't be alone when God is right in this with you. God will send you friends and associates, whatever you need, but it will be right for you. God will embrace you and uplift you instead of attempting to make you small and hidden to all, including yourself.

You must operate in a sound mind. Doubt cannot stay - no more back and forth. Decide just one way. There can be no more saying, *I think I can leave; I think I can survive on my own*. There can be no more of this doubt. Start saying, *I will leave and I will be more than alright*. You survived this far. You've already proven you are a survivor.

The other verse I want to share with you is James 1: 6-8 *(KJV)*.

But let him ask in faith, nothing wavering. For he that wavereth is like a wave of the sea driven with the wind and tossed. For let not that man think that he shall receive any thing of the Lord. A double minded man is unstable in all his ways.

Rid yourself of doubt. I know what it feels like to have feared going home to ask for help. Those at home doubt you and choose not to believe that you are serious about wanting to be free. I know what it feels like to be afraid to go home to your parent's home, afraid they will not understand and pass judgment on you.

To you who are helping your loved one, it is very important in this stage that you do not doubt them. Yes, it's very important that you ensure that they are serious about wanting your help and very important that they do not take your love and help for granted. Please do not pump out doubt and fear; don't tell them what they cannot do. Instead tell them what they can do and what they do well. Their freedom and answers come through acknowledgment of what they can do and what they can do well, not what they cannot do or do not do well.

Your position here is to pray for them. Pray against the spirits and thoughts of doubt and fear, depression and anxiety, hopelessness and lack of confidence. Pray that they believe in themselves and that they continue to grow in their relationship with God. Pray that they trust God with their situation.

To those amongst the wolves, do not focus on what people will think of you. No matter what, keep goals in front of you that bring healthy results to forward advancement. Speak nothing but good things about yourself and others. Tell yourself you can make it. It helps to write yourself a love letter telling yourself you will get through; you're going to do an awesome job today. You're going to take down whatever giant that presents itself. Speak good things over your circumstances, yourself, your family and your financial situation. See the good in everything, no matter what. Speak life into your situation, not death. Believe you're coming out without any doubt or negativity.

NONE OF MY FAMILY

None of my family will believe that I want to be free anyway. Where can I run? Dad told me to never come back. I am not wanted even amongst my family. Even if I am they do not understand, nor try to understand. They only judge me. Maybe I won't go back to family or friends at all. Maybe I just need to stay away from the old. Maybe I need new land and new environment.

Thoughts like these can fill your mind when you're someone amongst the wolves. Many times, you may be challenged by either staying stuck or stagnant in moving forward due to worrying about what family will say.

Don't focus on what your family is going to think or say about you. Some of your family may fail to realize that you were in bondage. It hurts when you have family you love but they do not understand the bondage that comes with being amongst the wolves. That is my purpose for writing this book: to help family members understand what it is like to be amongst wolves.

Some family members form resentment in their hearts because you did not leave the situation or relationship when they advised you to or told you how. Many of our family members develop disbelief in us because we didn't leave in the manner or timing they felt we could have. Some family members hold resentment because they tried to help you through the process of leaving and you went back amongst the wolves or would not take their advice. They may feel like they've given too many chances while hoping you would see things the way they saw them; they feel you failed to see the wolves the way they saw them and they may not want to believe that you are really coming home this time.

You may not even have your family door to knock on, but hold your head up high and don't be concerned about what they're going to think. You have to move by action because many times we stop due to thinking too hard that our family is not going to believe that we really want freedom and we let that keep us amongst the wolves. We spend time replaying in our minds that there is really no place for us to go. We think of how our family doesn't want us around or how they won't give us a chance. We remember that while we seek freedom, they speak of how we are not serious this time. We think of how they sometimes speak doubt and fear back into us after we've tried all night to get out of doubt and fear.

I speak again to the family members of those who have been amongst the wolves: please don't do your loved one like this. The faith and the hope that they built took all night, sometimes years, sometimes what seems like a lifetime. The faith and hope they have may be so little; please don't steal the little faith that may have taken all night to build. If they say they're coming back home to recover, believe them if they really want help.

At first you could never really see that a person is in bondage. They desire to come out of a bad situation, but when they are in bondage their feet are stuck. So although they try to go, they're stuck. They wanted to leave and they wanted freedom, but they were in bondage. So this time, before you say that your loved one really doesn't want freedom, check and see if their mind is in that same bondage as the very first or many other times they've said they were ready to go and were leaving.

To you amongst the wolves, I know you may be saying, *where would I go? All I really have is my family, but they don't even welcome me back.* And some say, *even if my family welcomed me back, they won't understand my situation.* So you think about how hard it is to be around people who don't even have the wisdom or knowledge to have empathy for your situation.

I want to talk to you about the type of people to run to after you have been amongst the wolves in the chapter How to Leave. When first leaving, you may not be able to see how everything is going to work out, so you may see your choices as very limited. Take one step and God will make many more. Trust in God. He will cause people to open doors for you, cause your eyes to see where to go. He will show you more options, even give you choices. Trust Him. Pray and confess all your concerns to him. Don't you dare doubt whether God hears your prayer or your thoughts. He is all knowing, all seeing, everywhere at one time. Yes, He hears and sees everything. Nothing gets past God.

SITUATIONS TO OUTLAST

When you've been amongst wolves, there are some things you may have to deal with when you want out; I'd like you to be aware.

With family and friends, some think you don't deserve to be received back, as if you should not receive the same things as others. This is the plot of the enemy. You keep on going. Refer to the story of The Prodigal Son. Jesus tells the story of a man who has two sons. The younger son asks his father to give him his portion of the family estate as an early inheritance. Once the prodigal son receives the inheritance he wastes his fortune on wild living. When his money runs out a severe famine hits and then he returns home to his father. His own brother feels that he doesn't deserve to be joyfully welcomed back by their father.

You may have family members who think you don't deserve to be welcome like they are welcome. It is not about the deserving part nor is it about comparisons; don't let the enemy pull you into this. The brother wanted to compare, but the father went by who they were; both were his sons. Although the prodigal son left and messed up, the father called them both sons. When the prodigal son says he is not worthy, the father says he is still his son and celebrates his safe return. You may not feel worthy, but you are still God's child. Let God do the talking; do not get into this with family or friends. The father said son; he didn't say he was less nor did he treat him as less. He called him by who he was, regardless of his current situation or his past. The Father, our Heavenly Father, always wants us to know truth. Trust the Father. Rely on him. Pray because there will be those who do not want to understand nor want you to be privileged or treated well.

Keep your head high. Go by what God says and keep moving. God is bringing you out from amongst wolves to great freedom. There, you may have to face all kinds of hatred from people who feel you are undeserving. There may be negative speakers, joy stealers, naysayers; everyone will not be happy about your freedom. Stay close to the Father and let him minister to you like never before. The safest place is with the Father. Pray and talk with the Heavenly Father often.

To those with a loved one in this stage, don't allow anyone to treat the one coming home like they are less than the others. They must know who they are. Tell them who they are. Celebrate that they just barely made it home and embrace them.

HOW TO LEAVE

Before we can get into discussion about how to leave, the first step is identifying where to go. Many times, this is done incorrectly when one makes the decision to knock at the wrong door. You want to go where you can be helped. Accepting wrong invites will be critical coming from amongst the wolves. Not obtaining the proper help can result in going back amongst the wolves. You don't want to go back amongst wolves. You may not survive this time, so stay free of wolves and the environments of wolves.

It is important that those you go to for help, whether it's for advice or a place to live, have a heart that is right for you. They must desire to see the best for you and your life. Beware of thinking that just because they have a heart for your children or someone else you know that they automatically have a heart and good intentions for you; it does not mean they have good intentions toward you. The truth is that the person can have a good heart and intent toward your children but not toward you. When their intent is not right this results in more pain, and you need to heal from pain, not accumulate more.

The person and the environment they're in need to be a good fit for your situation. The person must be able to accept the truth completely. The person you trust should not be prideful, not boastful, not selfish, not self-centered, not arrogant, and not controlling. They should be concerned about your healing; they can't be stuck on themselves. Their character must include compassion and sympathy for your situation. They must have the ability to nurture and give you the care that you need.

Going to someone who is barely able to care for themselves isn't a good idea. Don't go there unless God tells you to do so, because stability promotes healing more quickly. Trusting the right people helps you avoid leaving one group of wolves just to go to another group of wolves. You leave by going to a good place where you can heal, where you will be embraced and celebrated.

Surround yourself around people who are on one accord with you. How can the two of you walk together unless you agree? You don't want someone going to the wolves you just got free from, telling the wolves your every move and thinking they aren't doing harm. You need a well-balanced person, of much love, one having the heart of an intercessor. They can't help but to pray about everything and you see results from their prayers. You also need someone with

Integrity who loves themselves and has a genuine love for other people.

As you work to decide the best place to go for help, be honest about the danger that people may be in for helping you and work to keep them safe. The best action plan is taking safety precautions. You may need restraining orders; get them for other people around you too. Protect those that are helping you in freedom; at times they are targets for retaliation. Separate yourself from wrong influences; leave with nothing if you have to. Don't accept anything over your freedom; that includes money, people, and the desire for love. Don't stay for more opportunities to demand that the wolves love you how you know you should be loved by someone who claims to love you.

Now that you know more about where to go and where not to go, it's time to share with you some of what happened when I left from amongst wolves. I felt the importance of giving you a picture as I wrote to you how I left. My intention is that you be able to picture my story in your heads. I will also give you instructions based on what I did, as I have had to escape more than one wolf and these strategies were used each time. They work when they are truly applied.

Picture a sheep in a corner being bitten and cut. Well what happens when you corner a sheep and begin to bite and cut the sheep is automatically it cries out for help. Its identity automatically comes out. That is exactly what happened to me. I got cornered and my identity automatically came out without planning or thought. If you corner a sheep and begin to bite and cut, the sheep automatically does what it was made to do; it says, *Help, Father. Abba Father*... Its identity automatically comes out.

Maybe that's why God allows us to be pushed into the corner in the first place. Who you are has to come out; it seems your identity is discovered in the most challenging times. Some of us don't learn our strengths until we are pushed in the corner and some of us don't know how much we need God until we are pushed in the corner. When you get pushed in the corner, automatically without planning or thought, what's inside of you will come out.

I started crying out to my Heavenly Father for help. To those that are still amongst the wolves, and those who must win those that are amongst the wolves, know that in the wolf pack it's unacceptable to call on the Father and talk that Jesus talk. Some of you know what I am talking about because you are survivors of the wolves yourselves. But, when I got pushed in the corner, who I was had no choice but to come out. No longer could I hide then after asking for help. I heard the Father say, *swing your sword, swing your sword*. The sword is the word of God.

Before I went with the wolves, Daddy taught me some word. Then I learned some along the way when I was apart from the wolves, after earning their trust.

So the wolves were in an uproar, biting and cutting and hitting me - not physically, but spiritually. Then I started swinging my sword by saying: *Help me, Father. I am the head and not the tail. The Lord is my shepherd; I shall not want. I am seated in a heavenly place far above principalities and powers and rulers of darkness of this world and spiritual wickedness in high places. I am perfectly and wonderfully made.* See? I didn't have a lot of word, but I had enough.

You see it didn't matter what I knew or did not know; the faith to believe that God could and would save me was enough for God to move on my behalf and do what I could not. This began to cause some of the wolves to withdraw and give up; some began to wound each other amongst themselves. They were scattered all over the place and I was okay. Of course this took more than a day of speaking God's word and decreeing and making declarations.

Consequently, the wolves left me and went into discussion of the matter with the other wolves and Satan. Then Satan came back himself. Angry, he came to see if I was really free and there was nothing he could do.

This is the strategy for the one that is still amongst the wolves: cry out to God, fully committed, so that when the enemy comes back to do his check he says there is nothing we can do.

See I had been with the wolves so long that I thought my identity would never be found, but once you find your identity you find your authority also. So then Satan was angry, making accusations as if I had betrayed them. I knew it was God that saved me.

So the next strategy is to stay in a praise because the enemy comes back to see if he can do anything to bring you back or kill you this time. I went in a praise telling God, *thank you for saving me*. So when the enemy came he backed off and didn't want to have anything to do with me. My praise was too sharp of a weapon. Listen: the enemy came on other attempts, disguised and camouflaged, but couldn't stay. The atmosphere was filled with praise and worship on a daily basis. It went up as a sweet savoring smell to God. We were made to praise God.

So for those that are still amongst the wolves get your praise on. Fill the atmosphere with praise. Get your praise on. I don't care if you've got to praise through a dance. Praise Him with the joyful noise. I began singing *Praise is What I Do*, by William Murphy, *and The Best in Me,* by Marvin Sapp. No longer could the wolves stay close to me or enjoy spying on me. The praise and worship was too much. The praise brought me into a relationship with the Father. Your praise is powerful. God demands us to praise for our own good.

Once my relationship with God the Father increased more, the enemy was mad and wanted revenge to retaliate because of my freedom. They wanted to blame me for what I was not even responsible for; I only let out what was inside of me by being who I always was.

So through the relationship with the Father, He told me to not lay my sword down and that a high level of spiritual warfare was required. This is how you can come from amongst the wolves and live to tell the story. Pay attention, because if you are not amongst wolves yourself, your loved ones may be, either now or later. You need the strategy to assist them in becoming free; there will be some you can get to easier than others, so the use of strategies will be a must. In either case, there is a part for those that are amongst the wolves. They must do it; they have to be in action also.

So the Father taught me to fast, pray, to spend

time with Him to get the answers and instructions on how to carry out actions and fellowship with His sent ones, called ones, appointed ones, and get fed with the word and teachings of God.

So when the enemy came back he was already defeated before he returned. When he was spying he didn't see the greater strategy of the spiritual warfare the Father was teaching me. So at the time he came, I was well prepared. I knew how to swing my sword effectively, knowing when to swing it and just where to swing and point it. With the word of God and prayer, I connected with some more believers and came into agreement. God had me equipped and well prepared with others.

I joined with many of God's sent, called and appointed and got fed and loved at a church called Faith Healing and Anointing Temple in Tallahassee, Florida. They became my family and loved me regardless of my distance. I was taught how to love by the wolves so I was terrified to love freely and was still in the process of regaining my identity. I would sit in the very back of the church, last row, closer to the exit, and leave just before church was over. That way I didn't have to engage or develop any relationships at this time. I was still terrified to love freely and was not talkative at all.

Understand that I am very quiet-like naturally; I am introverted but can be extroverted at times, especially when preaching, in my profession of work, or when something happens, like music coming on. When I work in the industry of property management, I am an extrovert, or when helping other people (majorly when I sense the need of others to regain identity, but it is not limited to these few listed). I was very withdrawn at this point, but they did not judge me; I believe they saw and loved me from my end results, as if I had arrived to the point of having no stains, blemishes or wrinkles.

This is how those amongst wolves should feel when they reach your presence. It put joy in my spirit many days that they knew how to deal with me, although there were many that did not. These would ask why I was so quiet, call me anti-social or weird, or say I was mean; they said all kinds of things because they did not understand me. But I had finally found a group of those that did not judge me, did not ask me to change, question my personality or demand I carry a certain personality in order for them to love and accept me. God wanted things to change within me, but not my personality.

I was so happy that they did what God was teaching me in my personal times with Him. They openly praised and worshipped without shame or fear for all to see. I loved this. It was what I loved to do but they did this publicly with a joyful noise. I would say I love that they are not ashamed to praise openly. At this time, I would only praise at home; now I do what they do - openly, publicly, without thought or planning. I give God an *I don't care who's looking or listening* praise. I don't miss out on my praise time or worship. I take praise breaks often throughout every day.

The more I spent time with God, the more healing I obtained from the stinking thinking I learned while in improper relationships with wolves. The more I would trust to talk with these people and let them in my heart, I was convinced by their actions they were not out to hurt me. They were here to help, but because I was taught how to love while being around wolves, I was so cautious of people.

People who have learned to love amongst wolves do not trust so easily; they think at any minute something is going to happen wrong. It never happened. They continue to give my kids and myself great acceptance and love. My kids were begging me to take them to the church; they were being healed by the power of God also. God set me free greatly using these vessels to show me His love. God used their character and love to demonstrate His character and love toward me. They accepted me how I was but they knew I would change. I think deep down they knew that I would come to fully embrace the love they were releasing and become more open to all of what God was calling me to be.

When I go to visit them now, I sit in the front. I am open. I share and talk, and it's awesome to be with them. I drive hours to see them. I thank God for them. I pray there are more ready advocates like them, fully prepared and equipped to deal with those that have been taught how to love by wolves.
So to those who are still amongst the wolves, here is the strategy that you must do on your part:

1. Cry out to God for help.
2. Use your sword, learn more word.
3. Praise and worship daily at a high level in spirit and in truth.

   John 4:24 (KJV)
   God is a Spirit: and they that worship him must worship him in spirit and in truth.

4. Fast and Pray.
5. Get equipped for the higher level of spiritual warfare and get with other prayer warriors and believers of Christ who know how to pray with strategy and learn from them.
6. Stay under the care of your shepherd. Go where your shepherd goes, for a true

shepherd leads the flock to the Father. Let the shepherd's people be your people, and your shepherd's God be your God.

Those taught how to love by characteristics as wolves are terrified to love freely and fearlessly. What you do for them you can't do in all words. They have to be shown. Remember to love at the end results, not the current. Love them at the arrival, as if they are already without stains, blemishes, spots or wrinkles. By doing so you set a mark for them they reach to become. If you see them from the current, you set them with the mark to be where they are.

STEPPING OUT

It is very important that you leave from amongst the wolves unto a healthy environment. Some may not want to associate with you.

You see Paul had been amongst the wolves so long that he smelled like the wolves and no one wanted to deal with him. They couldn't see him at the end state but at his past. You may have to face this to. There were people God had available to deal with Paul and to help Paul. God will do this for you also. God will have readily available people to deal with you.

God will lead you where to go. It may not make any sense to you where he sends you or how, but trust God. God will make provision for you. God will cause the right door to open for you. Just be open to change. God may have one place for you to go at first; then he may slowly or quickly send you somewhere else. Stay open, my friend, to the sweet move of God. Don't just look for Him to move on your behalf in one way but many. He will send you where He is releasing his healing or where He needs you to be in that season.

It may not make any sense to you at all, but trust God. Some may not be able to return where you came from. That's not a bad thing. God knows the purpose He has placed upon you and He knows the route to take you. When you follow His lead, though the enemy may strike, you are protected on every side. You are safe in His care. Step out from amongst the wolves where God leads you.

This is why it's important that you communicate with Him. Team with someone to pray with about where to go. Trust God and have faith in God. He will see you through. It is important where you step out because you need to heal. Healing comes in a healthy environment. Sometimes God will place you in a place where it seems you are isolated, but He shows your need to be with just Him at this time. Trust Him; He is protecting you. He knows when you are able and when it's time to not be just you and Him.

Rest and enjoy the seasons. It will all make sense to you soon. You may even want God to speed up; I caution you to trust His timing. He knows the correct timing. Do not question God; rather thank Him. Trust the route that He leads you to freedom, healing and restoration. As with the Hebrew people, God may take you on a route that you do not understand. It may even seem to be the longest and most difficult. Still, my friend, trust God.

God knows what you need to be able to move forward. He knows what it will take for the next victory. Be submissive and obedient unto His way. His way may not seem necessary to you at all. Trust Him; in due time you will see the necessity of how and why He took you the route He chose and you will be glad you trusted Him and not yourself.

Understand that the battle isn't over because you have stepped out. You are about to see why the enemy wanted to attempt to kill you amongst the wolves. Why he hated you so much. Faint not while you're here in this season, because the word is true. Galatians 6:9 (KJV) says:

> *And let us not be weary in well doing: for in due season we shall reap, if we faint not.*

God is a God of abundance. Keep going, not looking or turning backward, neither taking of the old ways of thinking that would take you back into bondage. The bible says in Luke 9:62 (KJV):

> *And Jesus said unto him, No man, having put his hand to the plough, and looking back, is fit for the kingdom of God.*

2 Peter 2:21 – 22 (KJV)
[21]For it had been better for them not to have known the way of righteousness, than, after they have known it, to turn from the holy commandment delivered unto them. [22]But it is happened unto them according to the true proverb, The dog is turned to his own vomit again; and the sow that was washed to her wallowing in the mire.

Don't go thinking you made a mistake and, because you experience hardship and adjustment to the newness, want to turn back around. God did not call you to go backward but forward. Move forward. Don't let anything stop you. God will bless what you do. So you must do, for the word of God says it is impossible to please God without faith. Faith without works is dead.

Welcome. You have stepped out from amongst the wolves. Remember that uncomfortable and unfamiliar are good signs here. The key to winning is to rely totally on God, not self or anyone else above God. Get the relationship with God that the blood of Jesus paid the full price for. Get the relationship with the Heavenly Father; everything else really can wait. Love Him with all your heart, soul and might. This is the key to fast progress. Until you do it there is really no need to ask for anything else. The enjoyment of everything is tied to this principle.

> *Matthew 6:33 (KJV)*
> *But seek ye first the kingdom God, and his righteousness; and all these things shall be added unto you.*

When you really seek God with all your heart, you find Him and an abundance of wealth begins to flow. God gives you revelation of who you are and abilities you have like abundance of rain on a hot day that is overdue for rain. I love you, my friend. Keep growing in your relationship with God and obtaining the revelation of His word. I am proud of your progress.

Step out of the boat and walk, not letting fear stop you. Know that even if you began to sink you can stretch forth your hand and ask for the Father's help, just as Peter did in Matthew 14:29-31. Suddenly and immediately, without thought, God will save you; just place your trust in Him. God will cause it to be where you can't go under from Him consistently bringing you over. He keeps your head above the waters no matter how rough it becomes. Nothing can stop Him; His love for you is too great.

DEDICATED TO THE WRONG

It is necessary on your journey that you search out the things that you are dedicated to. The truth of the matter is that we are sometimes dedicated to the wrong things, people, relationships, partnerships, dealings, etc. A dedication is a strong will or devotion. This is dangerous when you give dedication to something amiss.

This includes something that doesn't support you, something that's not good for you, something not healthy for you and any relationship that isn't good for you or your relationship with God. It certainly includes a mate that will never love you. Love them or not, they will never love you properly. Maybe they don't have the capacity to love you but yet you are dedicated to this relationship or mate, strongly upholding something that is not for you at all.

The person or thing can be good but wrong for you. The bible asks, *Can two walk together, except they be agreed?* You know you are to be respected, but the other person is set on disrespecting. You see when you need to save money, but they are set on spending. You are dedicated to obeying God, and yet this person makes decisions for you and others that are

133

associated with you without consulting anyone. Once the damage is done in the disobedience, you have to bail yourself out of any damages caused.

You need to answer things and people you are wrongly dedicated to by standing for the things that God desires you to stand for and forsaking those things that are not in agreement with His desire or will for you. Survey every area of your life, ensuring that you're standing for what is righteous, pure, uplifting and has a good return for you. Stand for what provides a good harvest and inputs real smiles on your face, not fake ones.

You have to be careful because the enemy can play tricks on our minds and emotions until the point where we are giving dedication to things, people, assignments, relationships and places that do not deserve dedication. It doesn't deserve a strong will or a strong power. It doesn't deserve everything that we've got, yet we're giving it all we got. We have to come from those places. These places often involve pride getting in. Make sure that we don't have pride because it causes you not to see correctly.

One of the biggest cases of blindness in my life was that I was dedicated to something wrong and did not know it. God challenged me one day by telling me to forgive my dad. I said, *I already forgave my dad*. God said, *yes you forgive him for everything he has done to you but not to your mother*. He revealed to me that I had a wrong dedication. I was dedicated to ensuring that no man would do to me any of the things that I saw my dad do to my mom. That was clearly wrong. This dedication followed me into my marriage; I was always looking for it, so that's when it happened. I would respond how I thought my mom should have because I did not understand why she would allow my dad to hurt her and still not stand up for herself. God revealed that being dedicated to getting revenge for my mother caused me to be okay with marrying people wrong for me.

It is important that we make right dedication. Do not make wrong dedication. Having a strong will to uphold something that is not good for you leads you in all the wrong places. My dedication to the entire wrong thing led me amongst wolves repeatedly. Take the time to soul search what you are dedicated to. Ask God for His help in searching out your dedications for many are dedicated to lies, to childhood hurt and to reciting all the wrong that has happened to them or others close to them. It helps to ensure we are free from wrong dedication like fear and getting even for someone else's pain. Pride can be the vehicle that keeps us with dedication to wrong things.

Be dedicated to things worthy. Don't stay in wrong places, supporting the wrong things and having the wrong attitudes, thoughts or motives. Ridding yourself of wrong dedication sets you free from going back amongst wolves once you're free. The wolves are okay with you being dedicated to the wrong things, but not those that truly love you. They challenge you to get over it; they challenge you to obtain the truth and not to live in falsehood.

Wrong dedication hurts badly, especially when you don't do the necessary soul searching. This strong dedication to wrong things keeps us amongst the wolves and causes us not to detect the wolves, even after the first involvement with one. Wrong dedication and wrong thoughts get us here because of hurt, pain, trauma as a kid, hatred, fear, and anxiousness to prove another wrong. Wrong dedication causes you to strongly support the very thing that holds you as a prisoner. You have the key to your own jail cell. You are the jailer who holds yourself captive. Step from wrong dedication.

Be strongly motivated about things that bring righteousness, goodness, holiness, pureness, mercy and meekness. Be careful; this can be tricky for many. You need to do this with the help of the Heavenly Father. He knows what hides and what isn't yet revealed and reveals truth.

Some of you truly don't know that this dedication came through as a child or when you were unaware. It came out of nowhere. It slithered in, got in undetected and hid, hoping to never be discovered. You actually thought you were doing the right thing. Removal of wrong dedication in your heart is part of your freedom.

PART 4: WELCOME HOME

THE RIGHT WELCOME HOME

This is a time of celebration, when you welcome the one that has been amongst wolves home the right way. The celebration continues on past the day one, first return when the welcome is done right. Sisters and brothers, we are going to win many of our loved ones from amongst wolves, never to return unto the wolves again. Know that you are special for God to allow one so delicate and precious to Him to return to you.

Let's be faithful with the responsibility; God has trusted us. There was much danger that could have easily prevented them from coming home ever again. It is great when one makes it home. Heaven is happy when one of God's lost ones is welcomed home, even happier when welcomed home the right way by someone He has trusted.

In the book of Luke, the bible gives a display of a right way to welcome home someone that was lost. Take note of the Father's welcome home of his prodigal son; it includes a celebration, embracement, compassion, listening, giving of gifts and immediate care of physical needs.

Luke 15:11-32 (KJV)

[11]And he said, A certain man had two sons:

¹²And the younger of them said to his father, Father, give me the portion of goods that falleth to me. And he divided unto them his living.

¹³And not many days after the younger son gathered all together, and took his journey into a far country, and there wasted his substance with riotous living.

¹⁴And when he had spent all, there arose a mighty famine in that land; and he began to be in want.

¹⁵And he went and joined himself to a citizen of that country; and he sent him into his fields to feed swine.

¹⁶And he would fain have filled his belly with the husks that the swine did eat: and no man gave unto him.

¹⁷And when he came to himself, he said, How many hired servants of my father's have bread enough and to spare, and I perish with hunger!

¹⁸I will arise and go to my father, and will say unto him, Father, I have sinned against heaven, and before thee,

19And am no more worthy to be called thy son: make me as one of thy hired servants.

20And he arose, and came to his father. But when he was yet a great way off, his father saw him, and had compassion, and ran, and fell on his neck, and kissed him.

21And the son said unto him, Father, I have sinned against heaven, and in thy sight, and am no more worthy to be called thy son.

22But the father said to his servants, Bring forth the best robe, and put it on him; and put a ring on his hand, and shoes on his feet:

23And bring hither the fatted calf, and kill it; and let us eat, and be merry:

24For this my son was dead, and is alive again; he was lost, and is found. And they began to be merry.

25Now his elder son was in the field: and as he came and drew nigh to the house, he heard musick and dancing.

26And he called one of the servants, and asked what these things meant.

²⁷And he said unto him, Thy brother is come; and thy father hath killed the fatted calf, because he hath received him safe and sound.

²⁸And he was angry, and would not go in: therefore came his father out, and intreated him.

²⁹And he answering said to his father, Lo, these many years do I serve thee, neither transgressed I at any time thy commandment: and yet thou never gavest me a kid, that I might make merry with my friends:

³⁰But as soon as this thy son was come, which hath devoured thy living with harlots, thou hast killed for him the fatted calf.

³¹And he said unto him, Son, thou art ever with me, and all that I have is thine.

³²It was meet that we should make merry, and be glad: for this thy brother was dead, and is alive again; and was lost, and is found.

CELEBRATION

It is in the celebration that we announce to our loved one that we know they had to endure some hard challenges but, thank you for not giving up. The celebration is where much is announced and confessed. This is where you who were amongst wolves meet cheerleaders that were cheering for you behind the scenes. This is where you have reunion and revival happens. This is where declaration happens. You start to know how well you really did as well as how much courage you really had that others only dream to have.

Celebration gives the extra thrust to keep pressing and keep believing, although you may have some tough days and trying times. It is in the celebration when you know that your fight was not in vain. In the celebration, there are doors opening for your forgiveness of self. One of the hardest things I find for us as people to do sometimes is the forgiving of self. Celebration causes fear to be challenged, shaken and killed, for it opens the door to realize that coming home was hard but worth it. Celebration reflects on the accomplishment of making it.

Celebration announces marks; it marks the beginning and ending of seasons and promotions. Celebration divides the old from the new; it announces that one season has ended and a new one has begun. Celebration welcomes, just as on New Year's Day we celebrate the welcoming of a new year and make a mark that the old year has passed. Celebration brings a reason to be content with that which has passed and announce closure and newness. Celebration brings smiles, laughter, singing and dancing - all things that those once or recently amongst wolves are deeply in need of. There is great love that is released within celebrations; it is the love that makes celebrations to be so grand to our hearts.

For those welcoming their loved ones back, love is what one amongst wolves has been starved of the most; to get so much at one time brings the revival of healing and confidence. Celebration is a powerful act of love to give to one coming from amongst wolves. Do not miss out on the power of a celebration.

I pray that you gain in celebration what you may not have gained in other stages of winning your loved one from amongst the wolves. I pray that divine relationships are built, restored and healed. At this time, I pray that your hearts are open to release the very acts of God that promote restoration and all that is needed for recovery of improper relationships with wolves. In Jesus' Name.

EMBRACE

Those amongst the wolves need to know the difference between being amongst the wolves and not. The need to be greeted with real love is great for those coming from amongst wolves. The need is also great to see quickly the difference in being amongst the wolves until there is no more desire to even associate with the wolves again.

A real embrace will embrace more than just their physical. They need you to embrace their ideas and help them open up to receive the help they need. They need the emptiness to be filled with your embrace. Your warm greetings and love are released in your embrace. It is in the embrace where they feel the love. Embrace them in your words. Uphold them like the wolves would never.

It is in the embrace where you single out the greatness of them being home from amongst the wolves. Embrace brings about approval and acceptance. Embrace starts happiness to form from the inside to the outside. Embrace lets them know that they have approval. It's a gesture of love and approval. It lets them know that you have not come to judge but to uplift. Embrace says, *let's get through this together.* A welcome home cannot be without a warm, sincere embrace.

Do not miss out on the opportunity to administer embracement to the loved one that has been amongst wolves. I pray you administer the embrace to your loved one in a manner that brings deep healing and opens doors to more than surface discovery of identity. In Jesus' Name.

QUICKNESS

The Father's welcome home includes quickness. Quick means to do something fast, to move fast, to be alert, demonstrating alertness, sharp perception, done or doing without delay and to move swiftly and with skill. There is a time that your response needs to be quick and with skill. When one is returning home from amongst wolves, you have to act quickly.

Notice it did not take the prodigal son's father time to think whether he would accept his son home. Notice it did not take him a long time to address the concerns of the brother. It is important that others are on one accord with you, that they understand why you do what you do in the manner you're doing it. The prodigal son's father quickly takes care of the needs of his son as we can see in Luke 15:22. Notice this was all done at the welcome home before the celebration.

> *22But the father said to his servants, Bring forth the best robe, and put it on him; and put a ring on his hand, and shoes on his feet:*

I love how quickly the father is in greeting and meeting his son from afar in Luke 15:20. Notice he ran; he was quick and he did not withhold his compassion for a later time.

> [20]And he arose, and came to his father. But when he was yet a great way off, his father saw him, and had compassion, and ran, and fell on his neck, and kissed him.

Those coming from amongst wolves need quick responses. They may call asking to return home or for help to return. Do not delay. You may not get another opportunity like this again to welcome home the one that was amongst wolves.

I pray that you will be in close communication with the Heavenly Father and know which situations require quick responses. I pray you use God-given strategies to carry out quickness. In Jesus' Name.

COMPASSION

A welcome home needs to have compassion in order for a loved one to last after the first welcome home. Compassion shows sympathy for the suffering of others. Compassion is an expression of love. Compassion understands that we are not all the same and we respond differently to life challenges. Compassion gives and not takes; it is important that you give support and protection in order for your loved one to recover properly and regain identity. Compassion is what keeps the togetherness.

In Luke 15: 29-32 (KJV), I believe this is what the father was asking the oldest son to have: compassion.

> *29And he answering said to his father, Lo, these many years do I serve thee, neither transgressed I at any time thy commandment: and yet thou never gavest me a kid, that I might make merry with my friends:*
>
> *30But as soon as this thy son was come, which hath devoured thy living with harlots, thou hast killed for him the fatted calf.*

³¹And he said unto him, Son, thou art ever with me, and all that I have is thine.

³²It was meet that we should make merry, and be glad: for this thy brother was dead, and is alive again; and was lost, and is found.

Compassion is needed to cry out to God for your loved one. I pray that you will be compassionate with your loved one that you will be with the compassion to the degree that is needed for those that God has assigned to you. In Jesus' Name.

CRY OUT

Cry out to God for divine instruction and insight on how to deal with all manners. Cry out for God to keep you embraced in winning those amongst the wolves. To those amongst the wolves, you must cry out to God also. Apart from God, we can do nothing.

> *John 15:5 (KJV)*
> *I am the vine, ye are the branches: He that abideth in me, and I in him, the same bringeth forth much fruit: for without me ye can do nothing.*

Cry out for His guidance and divine order in your life. Cry out for divine healing and restoration. Cry out for togetherness in all areas of your life. You need all things to come in to divine order.

Cry out for your loved one to come into God's perfect will for their lives. Cry out that they will respect the rules of your home. Cry out for the transition and healing process in your loved one's life.

This is a challenging season. Cry out how God leads you to. Cry out for how to encourage your loved one. Cry out for instruction on what to allow and what not to allow. Cry out for the correct adjustment to take place. I say cry out, for the bible says in Jeremiah 29:13 (KJV):

> *And ye shall seek me, and find me, when ye shall search for me with all your hearts.*

Those that really seek God shall find Him. You will really need God's help in this.

TAKE THE GROUNDS

Take the grounds of winning those amongst wolves that God has given you by utilizing the knowledge, understanding, wisdom and instruction God has given you. Do not leave the grounds unattended. Do not take a break from praying and seeking God. Govern the grounds; do not allow the enemy to come back and occupy the grounds.

Stay in prayer about all things God allows you to see. Pray and praise about everything instead of complaining about things God is showing you about your loved one that needs to change. Praise God often.

I know there will be things that attempt to agitate you, but do not allow it. God trusts you to show you these things about your loved one that need to be taken down, for you to stand in the gap for them and not be agitated or dismayed. Disallow Satan's works on the grounds that God has given you to win those amongst the wolves.

> *Ephesians 6:12 (KJV)*
> *For we wrestle not against flesh and blood, but against principalities, against powers, against the rulers of the darkness*

of this world, against spiritual wickedness in high places.

I pray that you will keep the full armor of God on and keep your stand to the end. I pray you will take the grounds that God has given unto you. In Jesus' Name.

PART 5: REGAINING YOUR IDENTITY

RELATIONSHIP WITH THE FATHER

It's imperative that we obtain a relationship with the Heavenly Father. To gain your identity you must develop and grow in relationship with the Heavenly Father to go past surface revelation. It is in the relationship with the Heavenly Father that we discover who we are and why. Learning your identity also causes you to know your place. The reason it is important to regain your identity is that when you know your identity in Christ Jesus, you come to know your place of serving within the Kingdom of Heaven. To attempt to move a person out of place when the place is managed in complete obedience to God is like attempting to move a brick wall with bare hands.

Coming into relationship with the Heavenly Father where we develop the ability to trust, we also learn why to trust. It is in trusting the Father completely that we begin to discover our true identity in Christ Jesus. We also learn the rewards of trusting and coming into relationship with the Father.

Your loved one coming from amongst the wolves knows they are forming a relationship with the Father when it matters to them what hurts the Father more than getting what they desire. Your loved one turns desires of the flesh down so that the Father's feelings won't be hurt. Before acting, they want to know what the Heavenly Father has to say. What makes the Father smile makes them smile.

Another sure sign of growth is when the love for His people increases even more; they begin to show it by loving those that mistreated them. This relationship will teach them to love self and others properly, to have self-worth, to know what to accept and to know what to reject.

I pray your loved one will regain their identity sincerely and obtain a strong and healthy relationship with the Heavenly Father. I pray your loved one will know the heart of God and what makes Him smile, laugh, sad, excited, and proud. I pray that your loved one will not miss out on the greatest relationship one can ever have.

WHO AND WHERE I AM

Not knowing your identity is what causes you to be easily lured by the wolves' schemes. It is not so easy to lead someone astray who knows their identity in Christ.

Discovering who you are and why gives freedom in areas you've struggled with and rids you of imbalance. It gives you the wholeness needed to face those things that once bounded you. You're able to smile and continue walking in your freedom, not affected by what once led you astray. You're able to say no without fear. You gain boundaries of what you will do and won't. You're confident the Father has everything in control, no matter how it looks.

Let nothing stop or dismay you from seeking God for who you are and where you are; God wants you to seek Him for the answers to all your questions. Jeremiah 33:3 lets us know that there are things we do not know. There's much God wants to say to us about ourselves. You must notice the Lord tells Jeremiah to call to Him and He will answer; we must ask.

> *Jeremiah 33:3 (NASB)*
> *Call to me and I will answer you, and I will tell you great and mighty things, which you do not know.*

Knowing identity opens the door for you to know your assignment. God knows who we are and why we are who we are, and He wants to tell us. In the bible, Jeremiah 1:5-9, notice God tells Jeremiah that He knew him, before he was formed in his mother's womb. Who on earth knows us before we are formed other than God? This is who your loved one must rely on to tell them who they are.

I love that God gives Jeremiah details; God doesn't just tell Jeremiah he ordained him a prophet, but He tells him that He ordained him a prophet unto the nations.

> *Jeremiah 1: 5-9 (KJV)*
> *5Before I formed thee in the belly I knew thee; and before thou camest forth out of the womb I sanctified thee, and I ordained thee a prophet unto the nations.*
> *6 Then said I, Ah, Lord GOD! behold, I cannot speak: for I am a child.*
>
> *7 But the LORD said unto me, Say not, I am a child: for thou shalt go to all that I shall send thee, and whatsoever I command thee thou shalt speak.*
> *8 Be not afraid of their faces: for I am with thee to deliver thee, saith the LORD.*
> *9 Then the LORD put forth his hand, and touched my mouth. And the LORD said*

unto me, Behold, I have put my words in
thy mouth.
[10] See, I have this day set thee over the
nations and over the kingdoms, to root
out, and to pull down, and to destroy, and
to throw down, to build, and to plant.

It is important that we be in God's timing of
when we do things in our lives. This is why it is
so important we know where we are and in
what season. Many do not know how precious
it is to be in God's timing of occurrences in their
lives. In my words it means to not be out of His
timing when special occurrences are to be
within your life.

You do not want to obtain anything before God
puts His approval upon it, before He has put the
finishing touches upon it. You do not want a
marriage with a spouse that hasn't allowed God
to finish His will to groom the person for
marriage. You do not want to go into business
before God grooms you to handle it and places
the right people in place to receive you.

> *1 Chronicles 12:32 (KJV)*
> *And of the children of Issachar, which*
> *were men that had understanding of the*
> *times, to know what Israel ought to do;*
> *the heads of them were two hundred; and*
> *all their brethren were at their*
> *commandment.*

Once you begin to know the truth of who you are and where you are in the season, you're in. You know more of what you ought to be doing, your divine purpose.

I pray that you will now come to know more about who you are and why, where you are currently and in what season, and what you are supposed to do within the season you're in, understanding the timing of when to do what you should when you should.

PROPER RELATIONSHIPS

To those recently amongst wolves, proper relationships are major keys in discovery and regaining identity. Proper relationships help you to walk freely in your identity. Improper relationships hinder and delay us in all areas of life. It is important that we are in healthy relationships. To those that are helping your loved one, pray for healthy relationships to be within the loved one's life and for God's protection from improper relationships. It is very important that your loved one learns the values of proper relationships. It is hard when one has never been in proper relationships.

Proper relationships honor your God-given purpose. Proper relationships support who you are and where you are going instead of violating. An improper relationship pulls us from our God-given tasks and drains us of the peace God has given us to flow freely in our assignments. Proper relationships cause us to continue discovery of identity freely.

One benefit of proper relationships is that they promote us to know and walk in identity, avoiding unnecessary conflict. As seasons change and shift with God's timing, in one season it may be okay to befriend someone, but in another it may no longer be. You must learn when the season has changed in relationships and be quick to make needed adjustments without complaining and needing all the answers.

I pray in the name of Jesus that your loved one will enter divine relationships. I pray for relationships that promote growth in discovering identity in Christ Jesus and holiness. I pray for you and your loved one to enter relationships that give unconditional love and that embrace your gifts, talents and God-given assignments. In Jesus' Name.

NO SHAME, NO HUMILIATION

This is one of my favorite parts to regaining your identity. I enjoy imagining people walking in their identity in freedom. When we deal with hidden feelings and fears that would cause us to have shame or be humiliated, we are then able to walk in our identity in freedom. You have been through too much not to regain your identity and to walk in your identity freely.

I am smiling because of the thoughts of those once amongst wolves walking in their identity freely, not held back, not on the edge, not hiding what they have been through or been involved in, but releasing how they got over it with others. When we share our trials and tests with others, it helps to free others. What you have done wrong and corrected can be used for the greatest turnaround in another individual's life, causing others to avoid what you went through.

Do not beat yourself up about your past nor let others; instead, use it to help others and stay free from what once led you from truth. Walk fully in your identity by not allowing shame to cause you to lock yourself up from others nor hide what is needed and intended to be released to others. Do not lock your testimony up; others need to know how you got over, how you made it through. They need to know why you are still standing. It's okay to fall down, but not okay to stay down. Get back up and walk out into the purpose God has called you to without shame or humiliation of who you once were or what you once did. Keep moving forward, not looking back into your past. Thank God you made it over.

To those that are helping a loved one that is dealing with shame and humiliation, pray they forgive themselves as well as others. Shame can go undetected because oftentimes it seems so easy for us to forgive others instead of ourselves. There can be deep hatred one holds toward self about what they have done. Your loved one must confront and deal with emotions that keep shame and humiliation alive. It's hurtful to fail others and even more to fail self, but we must forgive ourselves like we do others. We must understand that we are all on the journey of learning.

Repent for the wrong you've done, errors you've made and all the disappointments. Get rid of all negative thoughts you may house toward yourself and others. Get over it and live without shame or humiliation. Shame steals and causes us to close ourselves to things God needs us to be open to receive and release. I pray for soundness of mind and that forgiveness takes place in your hearts and spirits like never before. You allow God to deal and bring exposure of any hidden hatred and un-forgiveness toward self or others that causes shame and humiliation to not be released. I pray you walk in your identity without any shame or humiliation about your past. Be you freely.

HOW TO BE OKAY IN THE UNFAMILIAR

A lot of the time familiar places stunt growth, so it's imperative sometimes for God to allow us to be in unfamiliar places. He takes us into the unfamiliar places to develop us and to cause us to regain identity or to gain identity. Oftentimes in order for us to know who we really are we have to be out of reach of those systems and people it was so easy for us to run to. It is frequently our dependence on those systems and people instead of God that are the main hindrances to discovering our true identity.

God allows us to be in places where systems and people are not familiar. Amazing things happen when in the unfamiliar because you have to depend on God. You have to get to a point where you really start doing some soul-searching.

It is often in the unfamiliar places that we really decide to discover our real talents or purpose. Hear and seek God's voice for the answer instead of everyone else's; expect God. It's in those times we really begin to see our true value and our true worth. It's in those unfamiliar places we become unavailable to entertaining lies; we seek truth relentlessly. We realize nothing other than the truth will help. It is in the unfamiliar that God prepares us for our assignment. The unfamiliar takes us out of our comfort zone. Most of the time it is to a place disliked, where you are not able to use much of anything already learned or utilize any of the old resources or strategies. It's in the unfamiliar places that most of us experience and come to realize that we didn't even know who we were ourselves.

I encourage you to enjoy the unfamiliar; it takes time to get used to, especially when you are used to knowing everyone in your area or social circle and go to knowing no one. You want to connect with those you know, but you're thousands of miles away. Trust me; be okay with it. God is using the unfamiliar for your good. God has to move us away from all the distraction to get our attention before it's too late to help us avoid delay or something worse than just a delay. The unfamiliar is a place to really get into the presence of God and ask all the questions you never had any answers to. It is a place to really grow in areas once neglected.

The unfamiliar teaches us how to depend and rely on God. It teaches us that God is more than enough to take care of all our concerns and that all is well. In the unfamiliar places God develops Godly character in us and takes out that which is not good and molds in Godly character. God gives us mirror images of ourselves and brings us into agreement with Him on the flaws we need to change.

The unfamiliar moves all the distraction out of the way so that you may seek God for the answers and deal with those hidden issues that would attempt to hinder us in the future. The unfamiliar is the place God uses to prepare great men and women for greatness. Enjoy your journey with the Heavenly Father in the unfamiliar places, because this is the sign that major growth is needed and the unfamiliar is the place for the growth to occur.

I pray that you enjoy the unfamiliar places and know that God is not trying to hurt you but heal you, not trying to decrease you but increase you, not demote you but promote you. Use the unfamiliar to take advantage of the time it provides to rediscover and regain your identity.

ABOUT THE AUTHOR

Crystal Jackson is the Founder of Anointing on Fire Ministries, where she serves as a Prophetess. She empowers others to find their identity and grow in relationship and knowledge of Jesus Christ by keeping a place open via conference line for those locally and internationally by logging in to 218-548-3055, access code 7321#. Here you can expect God's teaching, equipping, power, anointing and fire to be released. Crystal currently resides in Florida with her 2 adult daughters and 2 sons.

Crystal is also the Owner and CEO of Synergy Recruiting Agency where she serves as Executive Director, helping clients and candidates in property management find the right fit and right outcome involving career decisions. Crystal helps nonprofit owners and their communities synergize with each other, bringing the greater good from the nonprofit to the community and community greater good to the nonprofit organizations with creative strategies. She also helps nonprofits obtain quality volunteers and helps volunteers gain new job experience and ideas to reach career goals.

Crystal enjoys uplifting others throughout their career journey on Twitter @synergyrecruit2 and Periscope.

Websites: anointingonfire.org and synergyrecruitingagency.com

You can follow Crystal:
Twitter: @SynergyRecruit2 and @anointingonfire
Facebook: Crystal Jackson
Google+: anointingonfire
Periscope: anointingonfire

Visit anointingonfire.org for updates on other books and skits to come.

35643314R00104